YOUR GUIDE

Building Insurance

How To Select the Correct Building Sum Insured Value for Low-Rise and High-Rise Structures

MICHAEL A.N.P. CRETIKOS

Copyright © 2023 Michael Albert Netter Perandonakis Cretikos
First Edition 2024
Building Insurance Your Guide/Cretikos, Michael A.N.P.

Hardcover ISBN 978-0-6456528-4-0
Paperback ISBN 978-0-6456528-2-6
eBook ISBN 978-0-6456528-3-3

Library of Congress Control Number: TXu 2-391-714 Registration date October 04, 2023

All rights reserved. No part of this publication may be reproduced, distributed, or transmitted in any form or by any means, including photocopying, recording, or other electronic or mechanical methods, without the prior written permission of the publisher. Please purchase only authorized editions. Copies sold without a front cover are not authorized editions. For more information, address Publisher: IngramSpark self-publication and distribution program through:

Lightning Source LLC
Attn: General Counsel
One Ingram Boulevard
La Vergne, TN 37086
legal@ingramcontent.com

Cover design by Jennifer Stimson: Reedsy
Book design by Jennifer Stimson: Reedsy

The New South Wales Government supports and encourages the distribution of its material.
Unless otherwise noted, all copyright material available on or through its website is licensed under a Creative Commons Attribution 4.0 International licence (CC BY 4.0). This licence allows the sharing (copy and redistribute in any medium or format) and to adapt (remix, transform, and build upon) content for any purpose, even commercially.
For access to legislation in force in NSW, go to the official NSW Government website for online publication of legislation at **www.legislation.nsw.gov.au**

Copyright, Legal Notice, Limitation of Liability and Disclaimer of Warranty
This publication is protected under the US copyright Act of 1976 and all other international, federal, state, and local laws and all rights are reserved, including resale rights.
Please note that much of this publication is based on personal experience and anecdotal evidence. Although the author and publisher have made every reasonable attempt to achieve a complete accuracy of the information in this guide, they assume no responsibility for errors or omissions. Also, use this information as you see fit, and at your own risk. Your situation may not be exactly suited to the examples illustrated here; you should adjust your use of the information and recommendations accordingly. Meant to inform and entertain the reader, nothing in this book should replace common sense, legal, medical, or other professional advice. Any trademarks, service marks, product names, or named features are only for reference. There is no implied endorsement if we use one of these terms.
The publisher and the author make no representation or warranties regarding the accuracy or completeness of the contents of this work and specifically disclaim all warranties, including without limitation, warranties of fitness for a particular purpose. No warranty may be created or extended by sales or promotional materials. The information and strategies contained may not be suitable for every situation. This work is sold understanding that the publisher is not engaged in rendering legal, accounting, or other professional services. If professional help is required, the services of a competent professional person should be sought. Neither the publisher nor the author shall be liable for damages arising. That an organization or website is referred to in this work as a citation and/or a potential source of further information does not mean that the author or publisher endorses the information that the organization or website may provide or the recommendations it may make. Further, readers should know that internet websites listed in this work may have changed or disappeared between when this work was written and when it is read.
Material in this work and any other third-party material is licensed under the Creative Commons Attribution 4.0 International license. (CC BY 4.0)

https://www.michaelcretikos.com.au
https://www.manpcretikos.com.au

manpcretikos@gmail.com

ABOUT THE AUTHOR

Michael Albert Netter Perandonakis Cretikos
Image by Jazzy Photography

Michael's birthplace is the Mozambique capital city of Maputo, historically known as Lourenco Marques. He began his education at St. Peter's Preparatory School in Rivonia, Republic of South Africa, and later completed his studies at St. John's College in Johannesburg. In 1971, he obtained a Bachelor of Architecture degree from the University of KwaZulu-Natal, Howard College Campus, Durban.

Following the completion of his mandatory military service as a Second Lieutenant in Mozambique, he relocated to South Africa and began his professional journey with the South African Railways. He successfully ascended to the role of Regional Architect in the Natal System.

Having emigrated to Australia in 1988, he was appointed as the Architectural Strategic Facilities Planning Officer at The University of New South Wales. He held the same position at The University of Sydney until retirement in July 2010.

Following years of active participation in his strata owners' corporation, a significant underestimation of their compulsory building insurance valuation motivated him to investigate the issue. After several years, he produced his final manuscript in 2024, *Building Insurance: Your Guide.*

According to Michael, he is the creator of the BSI Value, which is established upon current rental values as the primary component for Replacement Value.

His recent foray into non-fiction writing has begun, with his upcoming book tentatively titled *"Strata Facts and Foibles."* Within this research, he will explore the complexities of strata legislation and building insurance, highlighting their substantial influence on the financial strategies of the Owners Corporation (OC) and the meticulous procedure of choosing the suitable BSI Value. He strongly advises that the determination of value should rely on both current and projected rental values, serving as the foundation for Replacement Value. It is imperative that the Replacement Value is increased to cover supplementary expenses. The discussion will cover the adverse impacts of legislative language related to auditing, insurance, levies, and assessments, along with the necessary 10-year Capital Works Plan, emphasizing the digitization of financial statements forming the Strata Financial Plan.

Michael lives in his home alongside his wife, where he writes and tends to his rose garden with grand passion.

Building Insurance Your Guide

AUTHOR BRAND STORY

I have always found myself deeply fascinated by intricate details, and my inner drive stems from the pursuit of distinguishing between right and wrong, as well as exploring the ambiguous territories that lie in between.

What adds to the relevance of this work is my gained understanding of the operations of strata owners corporations and the corresponding legislation mandating building insurance for such corporations.

This greatly emphasizes my role in uncovering, clarifying, and advocating for the rectification of issues pertaining to insurance and associated legislation.

During my tenure as the treasurer of the strata committee, I was entrusted with overseeing the financial plan. During this timeframe, a particular strata manager secured a renewal insurance policy with a value approximately half that of its predecessor. This individual was resolute in their belief that our OC should adopt the new, more affordable insurance. Notwithstanding my firm objection, they persistently criticized me and engaged in communication with the other proprietors, who subsequently voiced their backing, asserting that I was the only dissenter. I remained steadfast in my decision and subsequently embarked on a journey of researching building insurance, which also entailed an extensive review of pertinent legislation.

I hope my readers will join me in co-advocation for the changes for their rectification.

Dedication

This book is dedicated to my dear wife, Patricia. Without her support, this work would not have been possible, and I attribute the book's title to her. I also dedicate this book to all my family wherever they may live and a special thankyou to Jordan for assisting me.

"May you always have the wisdom to know what is right and the strength to chase after it!" Michelle Carter's *Seven Step Guide to Authorpreneurship*.

My special appreciation and unforgettable thanks to my parents, particularly my father, for affording me the magnificent education at St Peter's Preparatory School, Rivonia, St John's College, Johannesburg, and the School of Architecture, University of Natal, Durban, South Africa.

TABLE OF CONTENTS

ABOUT THE AUTHOR III

Building Insurance Your Guide
AUTHOR BRAND STORY V

Chapter One
YOU MIGHT ASK – WHY DO I NEED THIS BOOK? 11

Chapter Two
UNDERINSURANCE: ITS CAUSES AND EFFECTS 21

Chapter Three
THE BUILDING VALUATION SCHEDULE OF OFFERS 27

Chapter Four
VARIOUS FORMULATIONS FOR BUILDING INSURANCE VALUATION 37

Chapter Five
NON-STRATA GENERAL HOME INSURANCE POLICIES 75

Chapter Six
SUGGESTIONS FOR INNOVATION 129

POSTSCRIPT 173
ACKNOWLEDGEMENTS 175

Chapter One

YOU MIGHT ASK – WHY DO I NEED THIS BOOK?

Until this point, no one has cracked the formulation of an appropriate Building Sum Insured Value (BSI Value) to account for the estimated full costs that may occur after the Event.

I am concerned that solely relying on the conventional Replacement Value formula may not offer coverage for both replacement and supplementary expenses, which are essential for actual replacement and to prevent excessive supplementary gap costs.

The current array of strata titles acts and regulations have proven ineffective in addressing this concern. No regulations for general home insurance exist.

I assert I am the creator of a BSI Value based on current rental values. The unique aspect of this formulation method lies in its ability to provide a fair framework for allocating costs related to repairs and maintenance. It should debunk the myth concerning Lot Entitlements employed for such a purpose. It is especially suitable for high-rise installations with multiple tenants.

Why won't Replacement Value alone provide sufficient insurance coverage?

This is because the minimum replacement value shown immediately prior to the Event will not sustain and suffice for replacement and extra costs *after* the Event, due to the following reasons:

- Fiscal inflation from the valuation date to the end of the policy validity period and then inflation after the policy expiration for several years.
- Potentially increased building costs because of supply and code compliance, and/or
- The cost for temporary accommodation and expenses, which may not be compensable, either partially or in full, for the recommended minimum 2-year period for low-rise or minimum 4-year period for high-rise, to allow sufficient time for replacement, and
- Insurance policies have a validity period of 12 months, and the coverage for additional costs incurred during this time is often non-compensable or insufficient to cover the expected expenses after the occurrence of an event, potentially resulting in significant gap costs.

My aim is to enhance the readiness of property owners in case of a catastrophe, given that individuals frequently lack comprehension of the complexities of insurance Replacement Value and the Building Sum Insured Value they should possess to cover 100% of the estimated full costs and expenses that may emerge.

I advocate for legislative reforms to address the negative effects of insurance policies and current legislation that may bring about unfavorable outcomes for the insured.

I suggest a revision of the New South Wales (NSW) Strata legislation that includes safeguards for both the Sum Insured Value and the supplementary benefits associated with the standard Strata Building Insurance Schedule Offer line items, specifically for catastrophe and loss of rent/temporary accommodation.

To provide adequate coverage, this connection must include occurrences of destruction, catastrophe, total loss, and constructive total loss, for justice to prevail. The establishment of this connection through legislation is of utmost importance.

Similarly, it is crucial to ensure the safeguarding of compensation for expenses related to the accommodation safety net within the realm of general home insurance. Besides the BSI Value, a standard compensation value of 15% of the BSI Value should be the norm rather than the non-standard offer of say up to 52 weeks and up to 12% of the BSI Value for temporary accommodation, meaning the lesser value applies, both of which typically may not support and sustain the costs expected causing massive gap costs.

So, here's what happens with that current offer. If your claim is made on the last day of the policy validity, no period and no percentage value would apply. Therefore, no supplementary costs are paid besides the BSI Value.

If your claim was submitted at any point during the policy's validity and a "Total Loss" is determined, no additional expenses would be incurred since the contract would be ended promptly and only the BSI value would be disbursed.

The above circumstances mean that not only are the supplementary costs not sufficient for purpose, but compensation for them is unreliable.

Insurance Brokers Australia[1] (IBA) states:

> *By using our home insurance calculator to set your sum insured, you qualify for our Building Sum Insured Safeguard—it provides 30% extra cover if our calculator's estimate falls short.*

It is noteworthy that the statement lacks transparency and has not been cited in any of the home insurance policies referred to in this

---

1   https://ibacorp.com.au/avoid-underinsurance/
    https://ibacorp.com.au/personal/home-insurance/

book. The IBA website does not include any reference to it in the CoreLogic calculator for home insurance.

The calculator does not account for any additional expenses. It is the responsibility of the insured to select the BSI Value.

The utilization of calculators for structures exceeding three stories must not be implemented under any circumstances. My preference is for the complete prohibition of calculator usage.

After reading this book, the takeaways, among others, are:

- A crucial understanding that the language employed in insurance policies reflects a cultural inclination to deny reimbursement for supplementary or extra costs for both Strata Building Insurance and General Home Insurance.

- The lack of legal definitions for destruction, catastrophe, total loss, and constructive total loss undermines the inclusion of additional benefits or extra costs alongside the BSI Value, diminishing their promised values.

- Failing to harmonize Strata and General Home Insurance has led to an inadequate approach in devising a standardized framework for protecting the BSI Value and supplementary expenses, particularly in scenarios involving destruction, catastrophe, total loss, and constructive total loss.

- Typically, the Building Valuation Schedule of Offer's contents and values are overridden by the differing wording of every policy/PDS.

- Non-harmonized legislation for strata and non-strata applications avails this occurrence and usually makes the selection of the insurance provider based on a premium price, which may not be the best offer.

- Learn about the impact and adverse effects of improper NSW Strata and Commonwealth legislation on building insurance values.

- Failing to provide additional benefits for a catastrophe scenario due to the improper inclusion of the Insurance Council of Australia (ICA) Third-party Catastrophe Code or a state of emergency declaration by the State can have severe repercussions.

- The utilization of the additional benefits and increased expenses provision afforded by the insured by upgrading the BSI Value is contingent upon accepting the "Total Loss" proposal and receiving the payout of the upgraded BSI Value. Subsequently, these additional values included in the upgraded BSI Value will be readily accessible to the insured.

- The BSI Value is safeguarded by law exclusively in the jurisdiction of NSW. Unfortunately, this may be subject to the "Limitation of Liability" as mentioned in the PDS and mandated by the relevant legislation, which goes against expectations and may pose risks for the policyholder. In the context of Australian readers, I would like to mention that the NSW strata legislation differs from the legislation of the other 7 states and territories, as it specifically addresses the planning of the base minimum replacement value.

- Chapter 4 presents contemporary Valuation Tables for the Building Insurance Valuation Report, outlining the estimated Full Costs Replacement Value, with special provision for Architect Fees and Charges based on full costs, including provisions for catastrophe estimated full costs. It also provides supplementary information about insurance formulation for high-rise residential and mixed tenancy schemes, and

- The importance of employing varied approaches in formulating insurance and the relationship between data placement in the Valuation Table that changes and enhances the BSI Value during the estimation of full costs.

- The Valuation Tables provide evidence of the adverse and impractical consequences that arise from the implementation of the 80% Average Provision Rule in Real Estate Insurance, as demonstrated by the erroneous Section 44[2] of the Insurance Contract Act 1984 (Commonwealth).

- Irrespective of the presence of Mortgage Insurance, the provision pertaining to third-party beneficiaries in the above Commonwealth legislation's Section 48[3] possesses the ability to render your insurance entirely devoid of value if a bank or financier asserts a claim on your insurance policy for debt repayment, and that is whether you approve.

- The assessment of the Indemnity Value, a method frequently employed as a coercive tactic in property insurance assessments after the Event, is also presented as a solution for determining insurance value in cases of replacement on another site[4], subsequently affecting the BSI Value following the contractual agreement. (Refer also to Chapter 6 cl. 6.10 The Basis of Settlement of Claims, for detailed explanation.)

- Insurers frequently insist on managing the rebuilding process, which leads to the complication of the payout mechanism and its consequential value. If the owner does not consent, that procedure is deemed unsuitable, and I advise you to abstain from it. The longer it takes to receive your rightful compensation, the greater the likelihood of a decrease in your BSI Value, because of the proposed Indemnity Value assessment. Gap costs would significantly increase if this were implemented.

---

2   https://classic.austlii.edu.au/au/legis/cth/consol_act/ica1984220/s44.html

3   https://classic.austlii.edu.au/au/legis/cth/consol_act/ica1984220/s48.html

4   https://www.longitudeinsurance.com.au/app/uploads/2023/01/Longitude_Residential_Strata_Insurance_Policy_Wording_PDS.pdf Sec.1 cl8.1

- This could occur with replacement at another location or otherwise. The Law is not clear, and the "Limitation of Value" clause may apply.

- In New Zealand, the utilization of Indemnity Value Insurance is permissible where Replacement Value Insurance is not available. I disagree entirely with its philosophy. I do not go into the merits of that in this book.

- There is a conspicuous lack of legislation that describes a Building Insurance Valuer Practitioner, after the repeal of the Valuers Act of 2003 in March 2016. This may have a detrimental impact where an Unqualified Valuer provides a Building Insurance Valuation for strata schemes in Australia comprising 3 or more lots on a single site and title.

The NSW Statutory Building Insurance Value Specification and its link to the International Valuation Standards Council method.

Under NSW legislation, costs are to be computed based on the replacement value, regardless of whether it is a full or partial reinstatement or replacement. In addition, it is imperative to employ the cost structure method to achieve *at least the minimum replacement value*. This method is corroborated by the similar International Valuation Standards Council [IVSC] method. I will show how both methods could be improved.

The computation of Indemnity Value cannot serve as a substitute for this valuation, which may cause reduced values for partial renovation, reinstatement, replacement, or the replacement value on a different location.

According to the Strata law in NSW, it is not permitted to decrease the insurer's liability below the minimum replacement value. Failing to include the Building Insurance Valuation Report in the insurance contract documents as of 2024 has resulted in the unavailability of a clear minimum reimbursement amount. It is necessary for the Report to contain both the minimum and full replacement values.

The legislation's mistake is serious. Besides that, there has been an additional error in permitting the depreciation of the Insurance Value by stating that the insurer's "Limitation of Liability" may be under the wording in its PDS! Such wording is both irresponsible and prejudicial.

Including the Statutory Building Insurance Valuation Report in the insurance contract documents should be obligatory, rather than solely functioning as a means for brokers to present Building Insurance Valuation Schedule Offer options. This should not be done without first acquiring the customers' preferences through a proforma of sums insured values to be incorporated into the Schedule. However, Brokers shy away from this responsibility due to the extra work involved.

So much for the competence of Insurance Brokers catering to the needs of Insurance Providers rather than the Insured Customer and the lack of Insurance Council of Australia (ICA) standards.

To decrease the overall premium costs, it is recommended that the Insurance Contract Act 1984 (Commonwealth) specify only the sums insured necessary to be included in the Building Insurance Schedule Offer, as numerous values currently included as sums insured would not be utilized throughout the 12-months duration of the insurance contract. The insurer's aim is to give the impression of safety, ultimately leading to an increase in the price of coverage, which is already stacked with several statutory fees and charges.

The Declaration of Total Loss

In all building insurance policies, when a Total Loss is considered by the insurer, the contract is ended and the BSI Value is paid out, with no ongoing extra costs for rental accommodation, if provided before the contract is ended.

Where that BSI Value is for the *minimum replacement value for property replacement only*, that value will not provide support for or sustain the values required for *catastrophe escalated building costs, loss of rent/ temporary accommodation costs and expense, or statutory planning costs associated with that site* for a rebuild.

No legislation currently protects any of these additional benefit values or safety net extra costs values, stated in the contract, with *destruction, catastrophe, total loss, and constructive total loss conditions.*
I call for this to be corrected.

Who will Benefit from this Book

This book is aimed at:

- Every homeowner, Strata Lot Owner including strata owner's corporation, Homeowner's Association in America (HOA), Commonholds in the UK and similar community associations, including social and affordable housing providers and mixed tenancy entities.
- General readership in countries globally, Africa, Asia, Europe and the UK, Australia and New Zealand, Canada, and the Americas.
- Developers of residential and commercial buildings.
- Real Estate Agents and property managers.
- Insurance industry, including Insurance Brokers.
- Lawmakers, especially those who formulate Strata Owners Corporation acts and regulations in Australia and elsewhere.
- Strata and Property lawyers.
- Regulators APRA and ASIC that approve and allow insurance providers.
- Insurance Council of Australia and its member Insurance providers and related entities in other countries.

KEY POINTS

- The fundamental purpose of this publication is to counteract the prevailing culture of denial in insurance policies and, ultimately, to assist the reader in obtaining an accurate BSI Value. It also highlights the inadequacies in the legislation related to insurance and proposes suggestions for rectification.

- The insurers' insistence on managing the rebuilding process frequently leads to complications with the payout mechanism and the consequential BSI Value. If the owner does not consent, that procedure is deemed unsuitable, and I advise you to abstain from it.

- The occurrence of Indemnity Value for tangible assets in building insurance should be avoided since the Contract BSI Value pertains to the Replacement Value of intangible assets for real estate insurance. If you see the words "Indemnity Value" anywhere in your insurance settlement offer, head straight to a knowledgeable lawyer's office.

- In the event of a Total Loss declaration, ancillary benefits or extra costs are not eligible for payment, the contract is ended, and only the BSI Value is disbursed.

- Utilization of the additional benefits and increased expenses featured in the upgraded BSI Value is solely possible after disbursement, when these extra cost values built into the BSI Value will be promptly accessible to the insured.

- The insurance calculator does not account for any additional expenses. It is the responsibility of the insured to select the upgraded BSI Value.

Chapter Two

UNDERINSURANCE: ITS CAUSES AND EFFECTS

Factors affecting underinsurance are often the result of the data in the Building Insurance Valuation Report, if you are lucky enough to get a tabulated formulation!

Some valuers, including calculators, arrive at a valuation sum insured total in a few lines—no report table is provided, and maybe pages of disclaimers!

It is pointless and extremely inefficient to have different Strata Acts and Regulations across Australia for every State/Territory, especially regarding insurance clauses. What is the Productivity Commission doing about it?

Over-insurance, or the Perception of Being Over-insured

You should not be concerned by Over-insurance, even though Strata Managers are often paranoid about it.

It is virtually impossible to calculate *exactly* a BSI Value that will cover actual costs—including what amounts to be double rent costs incurred by ongoing management fees and levies (assessments) costs, and importantly, temporary accommodation rental costs until replacement is complete.

The value in the BSI Value is your responsibility.

The valuer provides **information**, not advice. Let the buyer beware!

The Escalation of Costs

Currently, escalation costs are invariably based by valuers on *activities*, such as *planning, council approval and construction periods*, and even *bank fees,* which are all entirely incorrect. This is because the insurance replacement value formulation is not like a general initial building construction project cost formulation, when first built "when new."

Further, both the IVSC and NSW Strata Act and regulations are inaccurate and incomplete in specifying the escalation factors, and I will show why.

A Fictional Case of a Typical Home Being Underinsured (This Applies Universally)

Let's call this case Molly's Loss Story.

Molly has a double-story home in the suburbs. She is insured for Replacement Value. Let's not concern ourselves with how she came about this information for replacement value. To make matters worse, Molly also has a mortgage loan on the property.

A severe rainstorm causes damage to the roof and rainwater pours into the top story, destroying the whole of the top floor. The bottom level is not damaged.

The insurance provider tells Molly the damage can be repaired.

Molly immediately arranges alternative accommodation, and the insurer pays for this comparable accommodation while the insurance assessment is ongoing.

The insurer arranges temporary repairs by ordering that the roof be covered for protection and then goes about sourcing a suitable building contractor to carry out the repair work. Before the contractor is appointed, another severe rainstorm occurs. This time, the entire building is damaged beyond repair, and the insurer says the property needs to be replaced.

This is when the insurer gives Molly the shocking information that her BSI Value is undervalued, and her property cannot be replaced, as there is insufficient value in her BSI Value to do that. The insurer ends the contract by declaring a Total Loss and pays Molly the BSI Value. The accommodation compensation also stops.

Molly is unhappy with this outcome and thinks she can sue the insurer for the extra damage to her property because the roof covering was not satisfactory, which she alleges caused the extra damage.

Do you think she has a case against the insurer?

Well, not really, because the insurer is not responsible for protecting her property or for any environmental event causing damage to her property. They are also not responsible for rebuilding her property—to provide replacement because she has Replacement Value insurance.

The insurer needs to repair but not replace property—that is the responsibility and the prerogative of the owner, and the owner needs sufficient insurance to replace the property and provide for extra costs.

So, here is the problem. No one ever told Molly that the replacement value insurance calculated before the event would not pay for replacement and extra costs after the Event. This is because costs rise because of ordinary inflation over time, and the extra costs are not built into the replacement value insurance value itself to pay for those extra costs, which can be expected if you cannot live in your home. The costs built into that insurance valuation are for Demolition Costs and for Architect Fees and Charges, and these costs may not be paid if the insurance value is otherwise exhausted!

If your home is destroyed, there may be higher costs after an Event to replace your home due to the severity of an Event causing prices to escalate. This is because of a shortage of supply for labour and materials and the scarcity of suitable rental accommodation that is like what you had.

Observations About Molly's Case

Molly has lost her home and needs to pay off the mortgage loan, leaving her with no equity in the property she formerly had. She also needs to fund the rental accommodation expenses for a long time—at least until she has enough savings to buy a new home again. Her wealth is going backwards, as the rental property is not gaining in value for her, but for the owner of that property.

This all occurred because she was underinsured—meaning the value of her insurance policy was for Replacement Value only.

What should Molly have done?

Molly should have taken the information she received as replacement value and increased that value by 30% to get the minimal 100% catastrophe estimated BSI Value. This might have saved her all the angst and discomfort. The premium for that increased value would not have been all that much—a few extra dollars in premium value, but a lot more security and value to replace her property and to pay for much of the extra costs involved. These costs are enormous in comparison. See the difference between a few extra dollars in premium compared to the huge rental value you would need, as described below.

While reading this, if you realize you are underinsured, please immediately get in touch with your insurer and ask for the policy value to be increased, as explained. The original contract would be replaced with a new one reflecting the increase in value of the policy, and it would be valid for the next 12 months. That will save you a bundle and give you peace of mind.

Here is the next best information I can give you. If you calculate that 15% of the value of your BSI Value will be insufficient to pay for temporary accommodation for at least 104 weeks, which is a reasonable time frame to replace your property, you are likely underinsured.

You should know what the current rental value of your home is, or you could look at the local real estate windows to see what the current rental asking price is for a comparable property to that which you have.

Say the rental value that you would require is $700 a week. Multiply that value by 104, and this will give you the total amount required for rental accommodation like that which you have for 104 weeks. This would amount to $72,800.00.

If 15% of your BSI Value is less than this value, you are likely underinsured and you need to raise your insurance value immediately.

Another quick check is to divide $72,800.00 by 15% to give you a revised minimum BSI Value. You may raise that value by another 15% to cover for increased construction costs after the event.

I hope that saves you a lot of grief.

 **KEY POINTS**

- Factors affecting underinsurance are often the result of the data in the Building Insurance Valuation Report. Chapter 4 contains examples of Building Valuation Report Tables.
- It is virtually impossible to calculate exactly a BSI Value that will cover all actual costs—including what amounts to be double rent costs.
- IVSC and NSW Strata Act and regulations apply the escalation factors incorrectly.
- No one ever told Molly that the replacement value insurance calculated before the Event would not pay for replacement and extra costs after the Event.
- Molly could not replace her home because she was underinsured—meaning the value of her insurance policy was for Replacement Value only, which did not account for extra costs associated with destruction and the extra expense of not being able to live in her house.

Chapter Three

THE BUILDING VALUATION SCHEDULE OF OFFERS

In this chapter, I show the values of offers of sums insured as depicted in Fig. 3.1 below. The terminology used for SUU is like that of CHU.

I frequently refer to two main types of strata residential insurance policies: the Longitude and CHU policies, as they are different in their approach to how additional benefits are compensated, and this is outlined in the schedule presented in Fig. 3.2 below.

CHU, Longitude, and SUU are different strata residential insurance entities currently available in Australia. Exemplars of rates for catastrophe, loss of rent/temporary accommodation are shown in Fig. 3.1.

Fig. 3.1: Residential Building Insurance Valuation Schedule Quotation Offer Showing Common Features

Standard policy offers	Expiring policy Longitude $4,929,560	CHU	Longitude	SUU
Premium payable		$6,320	$6,198	$6,691
Building		**$5,296,337**	**$5,296,337**	**$5,296,337**
Common contents		$52,963	$52,963	$52,963
Public liability		$20,000,000	$20,000,000	$20,000,000
Office Bearers Liability		$2,000,000	$2,000,000	$2,000,000
Fidelity Guarantee		$100,000	$100,000	$100,000
Catastrophe		$794,450	$794,450	$794,450
Loss of Rent, Temporary Accommodation		$794,450	$794,450	$794,450

Lot Owners' fixtures, fittings, and improvements		$250,000	$300,000	$250,000
Floating floorboards		Included	Included	Included
Flood		Included	Not included	Not included
Machinery breakdown		Not included	Not included	Not included
Voluntary Workers Compensation		Included	Included	Included
Additional limits:				
1. Government audit		$25,000	$30,000	$25,000
2. Appeal Expenses, common property Health & Safety breaches		$100,000	$150,000	$100,000
3. Legal defense		$50,000	$50,000	$50,000
Basic excess		$500 Ea. & every claim	$500 Ea. & every claim	$500 Ea. & every claim

These Policy Sections should be standardised in the Commonwealth Insurance Contract Act 1984.

Surely the below comments are sufficient for the ASIC and NSW Fair Trading, in any future Strata Act or strata managers act, to review the Building Valuation Schedule Offer common features and to make these offers, and inclusions, a fairer proposition for the insured and to eliminate double accounting or unnecessary scheduled items, loading the premium value.

By that I mean, the line items for "common contents" and "lot owners' fixtures, fittings and improvements" are *included* in the BSI Value formulation. These extra line items, as seen above, would add cost to the premium for nothing.

"Common contents" in this sense, means *common areas contents requiring work*, which are works items, as specified in the NSW Strata Act and Regulations.

Note: "common contents" is often misinterpreted as insurance for the owner's corporation goods and chattels, such as common rooms' furniture. These should be insured by another type of insurance as they are not building works items.

Another reason is that "loss of rent for common contents" is illogically misapplied throughout the insurance policy PDS by virtually all strata residential insurance policies.

Law should protect any Additional Benefits besides the base BSI Value, these being:

- The sum insured value for the Catastrophe Schedule.
- The total amount insured for lost rent/temporary accommodation expenses.

Each of the above schedule sums insured values is equal to 15% of the BSI Value, unless the catastrophe value is stated and shown as a greater value of 30%, which would be illogical because of the prevailing *declared* catastrophe clauses adopted. This means the catastrophe needs to be a "declared catastrophe" by some external to the contract Authority to apply.

Owners of a **general home insurance** policy will be subject to the terms of their insurance policy wording and conditions and is what the insurer wants to pay!

There are no standard scheduled percentage values that may apply with home insurance.

The additional value is referred to as a "safety net" and similar terminology, but it is ultimately determined and managed by them, and you are expected to agree or bear the costs necessary to meet your family's needs.

The location of accommodation and the value and period of that accommodation are not consistent and are what the insurer determines.

There are **no statutory Schedule percentage values for extra costs in relation to the BSI Value** applicable to **home insurance policies** in Australia, because the individual State Legislation does not include "home insurance" in the strata titles insurance legislation wording.

There is no legislation covering general homes insurance in Australia regarding the formulation for insurance replacement value and payment of additional benefits or extra costs value.

The General Insurance Code of Conduct **is not legislation**, but a voluntary code adopted by the ICA for its members.

Homeowners are subjected to the use of an **online calculator** to determine the value of the insurance value, which I would prefer if it were banned.

To be safe and to be guaranteed that the money for loss of rent/ temporary accommodation will be included in the payment, *with destruction, catastrophe, total loss or constructive total loss,* **or** for partial loss or damage, the **BSI minimum replacement value must be augmented by 30%, for both strata and non-strata applications,** so that **catastrophe provision values** incorporated into that BSI Value will apply, every time, when the BSI Value is paid out.

High-rise building complexes, in addition, require a greater period to account for the estimated **extended rental accommodation** needs, based on the total aggregated median or actual annual weekly rental values of all Lots of the insured building, **for at least 208 weeks escalation period after the expiration date of the policy** - being at least double that of the NSW Strata Act replacement value escalation formulation method.

Longitude and CHU insurance policies are compared side by side in Fig. 3.2. Additional Benefits are also referred to as Special Benefits in the CHU policy wording.

Commentary for the Axis Underwriting Policy is separately shown after commentary on Fig. 3.2.

Fig. 3.2 Differences and Comparisons between Policies for Additional Benefits/Extra Costs

Catastrophe condition	Longitude	CHU
Line items for the additional benefits values, as stated and shown in the Schedule, are values for "Catastrophe" and "Loss of Rent/Temporary Accommodation."	Subject to Section 1 Cl. 5.1 catastrophe. The catastrophe needs to be a **declared** catastrophe determined by the third-party State Authority, **and** the value of the BSI needs to be >80% of the estimated replacement value before the Event. *Note: There is no legislative formulation to prove these amounts! The building valuation report stating both the minimum Replacement Value immediately prior to the Event **and** the full costs catastrophe value estimate is not statutorily required to be conjoined with the building valuation schedule offer.* If either of the above two conditions/limitations are not met, NO Funding for Catastrophe values for **Both** escalation in building costs Value and Loss of Rent/Temporary Accommodation Value—if selected in the Schedule—will flow. That means you get zero for those two scheduled amounts if either of the above two conditions/limitations is not complied with.	The catastrophe needs to be a **declared** catastrophe determined by the ICA Catastrophe Code, which is the ICA Board Declaration. The sum prevailing/operative for catastrophe condition is up to 15% of the contract BSI Building Value.
Note: The *catastrophe* stated additional value line item, as stated in the Schedule for catastrophe, is normally up to 15% of the BSI Value, but could be a higher value, up to 30%, if selected, which is not recommended; rather, raise the BSI Value itself.		

Additional Benefits (A) for Architect Fees and Charges: *Note: Additional benefits is a dubious term and the insured needs to understand the policy terms and meanings they are dealing with.*	**Longitude:** These are paid providing the BSI Value is not otherwise exhausted. *Note: The value for Architect Fees and Charges should be included in the BSI Value—the contract BSI value. So, the Additional Benefit (A) is a misnomer.*	CHU is like Longitude except that Removal of Debris is also excluded if the BSI Value is otherwise exhausted. *Note: Values for* **Architect Fees and Charges and Debris Removal** *are included in the total BSI Value as per the NSW formula for the make-up of costs planning the BSI Value.*
Special Benefits *Note: Special Benefits is a term specifically used in the CHU Policy, instead of Additional Benefits, and is the same thing.* *Also, the term Policy used in this policy is the same as Section in typical policies.*		**CHU Policy 1:** Special Benefits apply for Temporary Accommodation Rent costs, including Storage and Evacuation costs besides your BSI Value. Under Special Benefit 1, Temporary accommodation Rent includes contributions for removal, storage, and cost of evacuation. The **combined** total amount payable is limited to up to the **percentage value** of the BSI Value. **Usually,** this is up to 15% **without** there being a catastrophe declaration.
Special Benefits *Note: Policies often refer to Common Areas Rent loss.* *I assert this is false doctrine, as this aspect should be covered by another type of insurance policy because Common Areas Rent Loss for goods and chattels are not "works items" and therefore should not form part of buildings insurance sum insured value.*		**CHU Policy 7:** Catastrophe Insurance. If selected and shown in the Schedule, you are insured *up to* the sum insured in the Schedule shown for Policy 7—Catastrophe Insurance—against the **Escalation** in the cost of replacement of your insured property if it is **destroyed** or the Insurer declares it a **constructive total loss**. a. **Special Benefit 1:** Temporary accommodation **only** is 15% of 15% of BSI Value. b. **Special Benefit 2:** This is 5% of 15% for **escalation** in costs for **temporary accommodation rent cost** due to difference in price of before and after the Event; and c. **Special Benefit 3 and 4 combined:** This is 5% of 15% for **escalation** in costs for **Removal and Storage** and **cost of Evacuation**—transport cost. *Note: There appears to be a difficulty in sorting those cost benefits and these benefits only apply IF the insurer agrees to them in writing AND after* **Common Areas Rent loss** *has been dealt with.*

Refer to the latest rankings for various strata insurance policies.[5] Note: These rankings change annually and may be affected by the number of policies available on the market. These rankings may not be true, and the reader needs to appreciate the contents of a particular insurance policy wording/PDS. Note: In all policies, in the event of total loss declaration/consideration, Additional Benefits may not be payable besides the BSI Value. I assert that this needs to be made payable through the Insurance Contract Act 1984 improvements.	Total payout will not exceed the Scheduled values for both Loss of Rent, and Accommodation costs being loss of the **Lot Owners' rent loss** AND **Owners' Corporation's common areas rent loss**. Payouts will probably take time, as individual values for each Lot Owner need to be worked out AFTER **common areas rent loss** has been dealt with. Possibly, the Consumer may need to foot the bill, initially, which could cause hardship and additional stress. *Note: The introduction of **common areas rent loss** will delay any resolution for the payment of **Lot Owners' loss of rent and temporary accommodation costs and expense**, causing gap costs and **loss and dilution** of total schedule value of loss of rent/temporary accommodation line item. No benefits will flow until completion of rebuilding, repair, or replacement on another site, when costs and expenses spent can be accounted for.*	This depends on the Catastrophe Code to be operative. The method to work out the values payable is complicated. Total payout will not exceed the **Scheduled values** for both rent and accommodation costs—unless agreed to in writing—which also includes resolving **the first loss of rent for common areas**. Payouts will probably take time as individual values for each Lot Owner need to be worked out in accord with any applicable lot entitlements. The consumer may need to foot the bill initially, which could cause hardship and additional stress. Funding could run out before returning to the rebuilt, repaired, or replaced property. *Note: The introduction of **common areas rent loss** will delay any resolution for the payment **of Lot Owners' loss of rent and temporary accommodation costs and expenses,** causing gap costs and **loss and dilution** of total schedule value of loss of rent/temporary accommodation line item. No benefits will flow until completion of rebuilding, repair, or replacement.*
Extra/additional funding: Note—Any benefits applicable will need to be first agreed to in writing by the insurer, AND after **Common Areas Rent loss** has been dealt with.		Refer to the above for Policy 7—catastrophe.

Note: Always consult the latest policy PDS. Please refer to the endnotes. Longitude residential strata insurance policy [6]

---

5   "Latest strata ratings" https://www.strataratings.com.au/ratings

6   https://www.longitudeinsurance.com.au/app/uploads/2023/01/Longitude_Residential_Strata_Insurance_Policy_Wording_PDS.pdf

CHU residential strata insurance policy [7]

Special note: The CHU policy has been revised since the above schedule was made. Date of preparation: 12 July 2023. Date effective: 1 October 2023. **Check the revised policy carefully.**

The AXIS Underwriting Residential Strata Policy for Buildings

The reason for adding the AXIS Underwriting policy besides those mentioned in the Introduction, the Longitude policy, and the CHU policy is that it differs a lot. The major benefits of the AXIS underwriting residential strata policy for buildings are as follows.

- Insured against accidental damage.
- Common Area Contents (*requiring work*). *Note: This is how it should be—automatic, as "common areas contents requiring work" are planned into the BSI Value as per the NSW Strata Act and Regulations.*
- 15% of the BSI Value for loss of rent and temporary accommodation costs is automatically included.
- Catastrophe protection option—up to 30%.

Reference to the APRA website suggests that this policy is not an allowed insurance policy in Australia. You should check that. I suggest that this policy should be viewed with a great deal of circumspection because of the complexity of the policy wording.

The catastrophe additional line-item value is up to 15% or 30% of the BSI Value, as selected in the Schedule as *optional* coverage. The catastrophe needs to be a declared catastrophe by the ICA Catastrophe Code announcement by the ICA Board.

---

[7] https://www.chu.com.au/assets/Documents/CHU_ResidentialStrataPDS_1023.pdf

Additional, or Extra Benefits as they call it, for Architect Fees and Charges, Debris removal, and Temporary site protection are payable if the BSI Value is not otherwise exhausted.

Temporary accommodation is 15% besides the BSI Value for Section 1, and up to **36 months** (atypical), providing the BSI Value suffices to support and sustain those costs for that period, failing which the insured is co-insured, meaning self-insured, for the balance of costs and expenses.

Rent is treated similarly and is part of the above value, but may also be "extended" for **2 months** after rebuilding completion.

Note: If the property is not rebuilt or replaced, the extended value is for a maximum of 36 months, which seems strange. Other policies state that without repair or rebuild, you get zero compensation for extra costs.

There are complications in settling the values for both rent and temporary accommodation.

The total payout will not surpass the scheduled values for both rent and accommodation costs, which incorporates the *loss of rent for common areas*—an assertion I consider inappropriate. Payouts will probably take time, as individual values for each Lot Owner need to be worked out.

The insured needs to foot the bill, initially, which could cause hardship and additional stress.

Regarding the SUU Policy, I advise caution due to its intricate language, and this level of care should extend to all insurance policies.

Provision of the Estimated Rental Accommodation Amount—Low-rise Building

The insurer's liability for Loss of Rent and Temporary Accommodation will be limited to 15% of the Sum Insured, unless otherwise stated by the Policy—it could be a greater percentage in non-strata policies (see NRMA) or the extended value with CHU Catastrophe clause wording for accommodation only, if agreed to in writing.

Note: The typical strata policy is not tuned for high-rise typology buildings.

 **KEY POINTS**

- These policy sections stated above, whether for strata residential or commercial policies, should be standardized in the Commonwealth Insurance Contract Act 1984.
- The NSW Strata Act and regulations state a few essentials, such as Public Liability ($20m) and Office Bearers' Liability ($2m). Other line items noted in the Schedule are optional and need to be agreed by the OC at the AGM. The broker provides a full list as shown and stated in Fig. 3.1. The full list is difficult to change at the AGM as the premium price will also change. Lot owners are therefore locked into paying for line items they potentially do not need.
- The policies for residential or commercial insurance differ based on the building complex composition, with a 20% tenancy percentage factor variance for each type.
- Legislation should make these policies and their respective Building Valuation Schedule Offers a fairer proposition for the prospective insured, by eliminating double accounting or unnecessary scheduled line items which load the premium value.
- A proforma of the clients' needs should also be a requirement in legislation.
- Loss of rent for common contents is consistently misapplied throughout the PDS of almost all strata residential insurance policies.
- Policies contradict when any additional benefits could apply and when they would be denied.

Chapter Four

VARIOUS FORMULATIONS FOR BUILDING INSURANCE VALUATION

The following examples are described:

- Table 4.1: The Single Home Insurance BSI Value shows a comparison between a calculator planned replacement value for my home and how the minimum replacement value is extended to account for the full catastrophe costs value, allowing for supplementary costs that arise after the Event.

- Table 4.2: The standard Low-rise Estimated Minimum Replacement Value BSI Value. This is specific to buildings up to three stories in height.

- Table 4.3: A potential High-rise 100% of the Catastrophe Estimated Full Costs BSI Value. This pertains to buildings that are four stories or taller. This valuation extends the NSW legal escalation period of 104 weeks (for low-rise) to at least 208 weeks, as I assert that the IVSC replacement value method and the NSW Legal structure method are useful for low-rise structures only.

- Table 4.4: My Innovative High-rise Super-Charged Catastrophe Estimated Full Costs BSI Value shows an original, unorthodox method for using rental values forming the BSI Value. It extends the accommodation escalation period to at least 208 weeks and adds estimated costs for code compliance for a rebuild.

The principles for acquiring an accurate insurance valuation are universally uniform, irrespective of your residential setting. This chapter provides an in-depth analysis of crucial approaches to minimize the financial and psychological burden that may result from an incorrect assessment of the BSI Value.

The tables provide information regarding the minimum replacement value and an alternative or additional value for the line-item inputs forming the fuller costs values in Table 4.2 and the full costs values in Table 4.3, that account for supplementary costs that arise after the Event. The variation arises because of the positioning of the input values in the table.

Tables 4.1, 4.2, and 4.3 describe my innovative method for inputting the Value for Architect Fees and Charges, so the input position of this value in the table has the effect of increasing the BSI Value to minimize gap costs.

In Table 4.4, the standard valuation methods are replaced by a new method that incorporates rental values as the prime BSI Values. This new approach replaces the input values based on building gross areas, including common areas contents requiring work, with rental values that encompass the previously used values and are aligned with current costs.

You might ask why I do not just provide three tables for single, low-rise, and high-rise? The primary purpose is to explain the fluctuation of the BSI Value due to the positioning of the input values.

The methodologies employed by the IVSC and NSW strata legal method pertain solely to determining the minimum replacement value for low-rise structures and do not encompass the assessment of "Additional Benefits" or ancillary or supplementary expenses. Nor do they necessitate their payment besides the BSI Value in the event of destruction, catastrophe, total loss, and constructive total loss, which I strongly advocate for.

Notes Regarding the Various Features or Metadata of the Traditional Costing Approach

The Initial Escalation Costing Period

The initial escalation period begins from the site inspection/preparation date for the valuation report to the expiration date of the current insurance policy. This aspect is often overlooked or inaccurately assessed in reports. As a result, the BPI cost rate is frequently overlooked and is excluded from the initial cost escalation calculation.

It is common for the escalation period for the gross building area construction cost rate to be undervalued. The combined gross worth should encompass all contents of common areas that require maintenance (work) to create the overall gross worth of the building, to comply with the current NSW statutory notion of at least the minimum replacement value method.

In its simplest form, the contents of common areas that require work comprise driveways, fencing, landscaping, and recreational facilities.

With a high-rise building complex, the *perceived extended rental accommodation costs* may be estimated to extend past the minimum NSW statutory 104 weeks escalation of costs period and should be calculated for at least 208 weeks, after the expiration date of the policy, as it will take longer to replace a high-rise building.

Insurance providers' PDSs are based on incomparable and unexpressed cost valuations, myths, and commitments that may require additional documentation. This reinforces my notion that you should be insured for more than just the minimum replacement value insurance so that you're adequately insured for the replacement cost and estimated extra costs, because they usually increase. In the costing framework for replacement value, costs allowance for living expenses is not taken into consideration.

The Second Escalation Costing Period

The second escalation period spans over 104 weeks for low-rise applications; high-rise applications require a greater escalation period factor of at least 208 weeks.

This escalation period starts from the end of the current insurance expiration or renewal date and *not* the commencement date of the current policy, as stated in law (SSMR 2016 Reg. 39), or the Event date, which are both incorrect because a claim may be made on the last day of the policy.

The Rule Known as the 80% Average Provision Rule

The 80% Average Provision Rule is nearly impossible to follow unless you're a mathematician and willing to risk being underinsured. I do not suggest you try to beat the Rule. You would be underinsured if you did so.

I want to clarify that you should **not** try to beat the rule by undervaluing your insurance value by lowering the 100% valuation to 90% valuation, as that might incur huge gap costs for you.

In a practical sense, the 80% Average Provision Rule condition is unworkable for real estate, and this is shown in the valuation tables and more explicitly in Chapter 6.

Insurance policies that employ the 80% Rule employ a speculative doctrine, which I say is unworkable. Where it is employed, it is unfair and not transparent. It is therefore important not to be concerned with the 80% Rule with *building insurance replacement value*—not indemnity value building insurance—and always select the insurance value for *at least 100% of the catastrophe estimated full costs BSI Value*. This value may be further increased, mainly for high-rise typology purposes.

Note: New Zealand may permit building insurance based on *indemnity value insurance* when replacement value insurance is not available, and this would have the effect of placing building insurance like goods and chattels or contents insurance valuation. Indemnity value insurance is extremely tricky, and the 80% Average Provision Rule may apply in the contract wording (PDS). You should have a lawyer beside you when deciding on the value of that intended insurance, to ensure you get the monetary value that you deserve.

Common Areas Contents Requiring Work

In high-rise constructions, preparing the value of *common areas contents requiring work* is significantly more intricate and encompasses the building's essential characteristics, such as parking, electrical generation, air conditioning, fire prevention systems, elevators, public amenities, and water and communications reticulation, to mention a few.

Please note that including the wording *Common Contents* in the Strata Building Insurance Valuation Schedule Offer, which is usually shown as 1% of the BSI Value, is erroneous and results in additional policy expenses with no corresponding benefits. This also leads to the incorrect notion that goods and chattels are insured by the building insurance policy. Making small claims increases your next premium with any insurance policy you select.

ASIC, Owners' corporations and Fair Trading Departments, please take note.

Frequently, the enhancements made to the building's modernization, common property amenities, and landscaping, which require maintenance, as well as the *fixtures, fittings, and improvements* added by the Lot Owner to the common area, are not adequately or precisely considered in the insurance calculation process forming the BSI Value.

The Calculation for Architect Fees and Charges

The sum provided for all Architect Fees and Charges, calculated as a *percentage of full costs,* should be at the lower end of the table and separated from the sum for Debris Removal costs, as the two *are not* calculated on the same basis.

In the Table Valuation examples, see how Architect Fees and Charges are escalated, so they *are based on **fuller** estimated catastrophe costs.* I illustrate disparities between the conventional approach and my innovative method of demonstrating these variations in values shown in the two valuation table columns—valuation 1 and valuation 2—shown below in Tables 4.1, 4.2, and 4.3.

These base costs for Architect Fees and Charges may form the basis of gap costs, depending on how underinsured the policy is and whether the BSI Value is of sufficient value to support and sustain the costs for Architects Fees and Charges and Demolition costs. You may recall that I said you may not receive compensation for Architect Fees and Charges and Demolition costs if the BSI is otherwise exhausted. It is important that Architect Fees and Charges are more accurately assessed to increase the overall BSI to minimize gap costs.

Finally, where the actual rebuild construction cost is greater than the BSI Value, with underinsurance, the extra funding amount required *to meet the full reconstruction cost **and** for supplementary expenses*, including accommodation expense, will be for the insured's account. See Molly's Loss Story above, as an example of the consequences of being underinsured.

Do not be underinsured! Insure for *100% of the catastrophe estimated full costs BSI Value*. This value is at least 30% greater than the standard NSW statutory method for at least the Minimum Replacement Value immediately prior to the Event.

Given the lack of more precisely calculated methodologies in other regions, I recommend adhering to the methods I have outlined in these tables.

Building Insurance Calculation for Part of the Building

It is not permissible to obtain insurance for a section of a building complex, solely to cover the Strata residential scheme, despite the apparent belief of the NSW Government and lately that of the Victoria State Government as well. Building insurance covers the entire building, including *common areas' contents requiring work*, because a building cannot be reinstated, replaced, or rebuilt in part only. The assessment made by NSW Strata Act Sec.162 regarding the division of payment for insurance premiums is deemed incorrect. This is applicable where the strata scheme pertains only to a portion of the building, and the Owners Corporation is required to pay the premium proportionately, based on the replacement value of the part (or parts) of the building under the strata scheme, relative to that of the entire building.

The problem here is: How do you excise a portion relating to the Strata scheme from the rest of the building when the strata portion depends on the key features of the entire building and these features do not form part of the equation?

In Table 4.4, shown below, I provide an innovative way of comparing high-rise building rental values—not habitable areas values—of each rental space component of the building, to arrive at a fairer way of determining the division of costs for repairs and maintenance. British Columbia and Canada, please take note.

Lot Entitlements and their Value Used for the Division of Costing for Repairs and Maintenance

The above is another reason insurance leads the way, and Lot Entitlements values, where they are not of equal value, are an irrational way of evaluating the voting rights of a single Lot or for providing the cost sharing for repairs and maintenance costs. Lot Entitlements in Strata are calculated on the sale value of the lot when first purchased and that value does not include common areas' contents requiring work, which are an essential part of the Lot and the whole complex.

In a Poll vote situation, this would mean that the wealthier you are with the value of your Lot, the more voting rights you would have based on that Lot's increased Lot Entitlement Value.

The Poll vote is used for significant occasions, such as the decision to end the Scheme or for determinations related to repairs and maintenance. This is indisputably contradictory to the principles of a democratic political system, where everyone—in this case, each Lot—is entitled to one vote of equal value. The percentage increase of the vote should not be determined by the monetary value and Lot Entitlement assigned to the Lot during its purchase, as stated in the Scheme's articles of registration.

"Lot" here means the space you own in a development, such as a Strata typology complex.

The concept of Lot Entitlements was initially introduced during the registration of early NSW strata schemes apartment blocks, wherein the developer enforced a constitution to allocate higher value to specific lots for the purpose of management control, and this system remains unchanged. I completely disagree with the system.

Four Levels of Building Insurance Value

To my mind, there are four levels of building insurance value, as shown in the valuation tables: Tables 4.1, 4.2, 4.3, and 4.4.

Table 4.1 for a single home is compiled on the same basis as Table 4.2.

Table 4.2 shows the Low-rise estimated minimum replacement value BSI Value and is the standard method framed by the IVSC for the insurance replacement value method mirrored in the NSW statutory method for the adding up of costs for at least the minimum replacement value immediately prior to the Event.

There is no distinction between low-rise and high-rise insurance value formulation described in the IVSC's or the NSW statutory method and both the initial and second escalation periods are inaccurately assessed!

Table 4.2 illustrates differences in input derived values shown in column valuation 1 and column valuation 2 and the resultant BSI Value is based on *fuller but not yet on full costs*.

Table 4.3 shows a potential High-rise 100% catastrophe estimated full costs BSI Value and is like Table 4.2, but Table 4.3 differs in that the Valuation 2 column shows how Architect Fees and Charges and the resultant BSI Value are *based on full costs*.

The exemplification of a hypothetical building composition, pertaining to Table 4.4, illustrates the distinct space components that could make up the high-rise building complex.

Table 4.4 shows my innovative High-rise Super-Charged Catastrophe Estimated Full Costs BSI Value and illustrates the *innovative assessment of rental values* for various elements or components, making up the high-rise building complex and their correlation with the BSI Value.

The market rental values are converted into BSI Values by applying their unique percentage relationship to the BSI Value.

The included line items are:

- Input of the rental values for space components of the building—x and y values.
- The initial escalation factor BPI Rate (Building Price Index) is in relation to the valuation report date and policy expiration.
- The estimated Demolition and Debris Removal cost.
- Code compliance costing—z value.
- Catastrophe loading.
- The final escalation cost factor of at least 208 weeks after policy expiration.

- Architect Fees and Charges.
- Addition of General Sales Tax (GST). The aggregate forms the Final Adoptive Amount (FAA) Value.

Note: The Preliminary Adoptive Amount (PAA) Value in this costing should not be selected as your BSI Value, as that value would be way underinsured.

Table 4.1 shows the difference in calculator valuation for my home using greater transparency of input criteria following the NSW legal insurance formulation method and shows the unique method to depict Architect Fees and Charges.

Table 4.1   The Single Home 100% of the Catastrophe Estimated Full Costs BSI Value

Description: My innovative method to provide the maximum coverage for Professional Fees and Charges based on total costs as opposed to Valuation 1 based on minimum replacement value.	Days	%	Valuation 1 Traditional Minimum RV BSI Value	Valuation 2 Innovative Catastrophe Full Costs BSI Value
1. Total building gross area of my home plus common areas improvements Total 141m2. Rates for medium level of finish. $2,120m2 2. Common Areas Contents requiring work; say 10m2 roofed deck and approx.. 10m2 retaining walls.			$298,920 $30,000	$298,920 $30,000
Progressive Total (PT-1)			**$328,920**	**$328,920**
Initial valuation escalation period: Valuation Report Date to Damage Policy Expiration Date period 31/05/2017-04/04/2019—based on time relative to the BPI over that period of days applicable and estimated 5% pa-formula: 5 x 365 + (x) divided by 365 - (X=no of days) > 365 over the period =428-365=63/365=0.17=5.17%	428	5.17%	$17,005	$17,005
Progressive Total 2 (PT-2)			**$345,925**	**$345,925**
Demolition and site clean-up: say 5% x (PT-2)		5%	$17,296	$17,296
Progressive Total 3 (PT-3)			**$363,221**	**$363,221**
Example Method 1: Architect Fees and Charges		10%	$36,322	nil
Progressive Total 4 (PT-4)			$399,543	$363,221
Final valuation escalation period: BPI increase over the whole reinstatement period is 2 yrs. **From** Damage Policy Expiration Date 04/04/2019-04/04/2021—104 weeks under SSMR NSW 2016-Reg.39—estimated 5% pa. Based on CoreLogic's BPI rates for residential housing in Sydney. Warning: Rates went up after the pandemic.	730	10%	$39,954	$36,322
Progressive Total			$439,497	$399,543
Plus GST		10%	**$43,950**	**nil**
Progressive Total 5 **(PT-5) PAA Value Min. Replacement Value.**			$483,447	nil
Progressive Total 5 (PT-5) BSI Preliminary Adoptive Amount (PAA) GST inclusive Replacement Value (RV) = to the minimum RV BSI Value as per SSMR NSW 2016 Reg.39			$483,447 Min. RV	nil

100% Catastrophe estimated full costs BSI Value (GST Inclusive) becomes the BSI FAA Value + Fees and Charges	+30%	nil	$519,406
Example Method 2: Architect Fees and Charges say 10% Based on full costs.	10%	nil	$51,941
Progressive Total			$571,347
Plus GST	10%	nil	$57,135
Progressive Total 6 (PT-6) FAA Full Catastrophe BSI Value includes extra costs and is the safest insurance value.			$628,482
(PT-5) Minimum RV BSI Value (PAA) as % of catastrophe cost (GST Incl.) or actual BSI Value PAA divided by FAA is = > 80% of catastrophe estimated cost. This shows how ineffective the Rule is. The higher the FAA is against the PAA, the lower the average percentage variance will be. In Valuation 1; $483,447 / $628,482 = 76.92% The 80% Rule is unworkable for Buildings Insurance Replacement Value.			

The report date should be the same date as the site inspection date shown here as 31/05/2017; Damage policy commencement date: 04/04/2018; Damage policy expiration date: 04/04/2019. Percentage figures shown for clarity.

In Table 4.1, the single home insurance valuation shows a comparison value between a calculator planned replacement value, for my home, and how that minimum replacement value is extended to account for the estimated full catastrophe costs value, allowing for the extra or supplementary costs that arise after the Event.

The Table 4.1 method is calculated like the Table 4.2 method for Strata in accord with SSMR NSW 2016 Reg. 39 that describes insurance for *at least the minimum replacement value immediately prior to the Event* but increased significantly to account for estimated full costs.

The single home 100% of the catastrophe estimated full costs BSI Value has inbuilt the extra costs that could be expected after the Event to obviate the misgivings of the minimum replacement value valuation. The reason for this is that the escalation period factor of 104 weeks, in the valuation calculation method, for the minimum replacement value alone, consistently cannot account for the supplementary benefits or additional expenses, such as the escalated building costs because of catastrophes, costs of lost rent, and temporary accommodation expenses that arise after the Event.

The insufficiency has arisen due to the restricted insurance value and the unreliable and inconsistent wording used in the Building Insurance Policy, which results in an uncertain payout for any expenses that are claimable before the policy's conclusion or during any period of compensation that is specified after the conclusion, which might also be combined with a percentage of the BSI Value, whichever is the lesser value.

This restricted insurance value is likewise applicable when using digital calculators, as the Replacement Value result will invariably lead to underinsurance and will not support supplementary extra costs.

Underinsurance applies to all general home insurance and strata, or condo or community (retirement village type) schemes' building insurance, where only minimum replacement value is selected as the BSI Value.

Notes regarding the potential use of rental values forming the BSI Value.

In its simplest form, the Weekly Rental Value for my scheme's villas (year 2018) was a median circa $700/wk./villa[8]. Hypothetically, the BSI Value based on a rental value for my villa thus calculated would be 700 x 104 = $72,800 divided by 15% = $485,333 + 10% GST = $533,866 BSI Replacement Value.

An additional 15% for supplementary costs should be added to account for *destruction, catastrophe, total loss, and constructive total loss*, for costs associated with escalated building costs and accommodation expenses for 104 weeks—a reasonable timeframe to rebuild the building.

---

8   https://sqmresearch.com.au/weekly-rents.php?postcode=2120&t=1

As a result, the augmented full costs total BSI Value stands at $533,866 +15% (escalated building costs over the period) +10% GST = $675,340 full costs BSI Value.

The calculated BSI Value is $675,340, which is slightly better and closely corresponds to the innovative planned costing in Table 4.1 above, estimated at around $628,482.00 using complex metadata—a 6.94% difference, which is negligible.

This shows the potential application of weekly rental rates in the calculation of projected expenses and values, resulting in a reliable BSI Value you should likely have. If it works for low-rise, it will also work for high-rise applications. This is further expanded and shown in Table 4.4 for a high-rise application.

The Calculator Replacement Value for my villa in 2023 = $518,679.00, as opposed to BSI full costs Value as planned and shown in the Table 4.1 above = $628,482.00 in 2018.

The value in the Calculator Replacement Value does not meet the costs of replacement and supplementary costs and expenses.

Table 4.2   The Standard Low-rise Estimated Minimum Replacement Value BSI Value

Description: My innovative method to show the minimum and a greater value for Architect Fees and Charges.	Days	%	Valuation 1 Minimum RV BSI Value	Valuation 2 Catastrophe Full Cost BSI Value
1. Total building gross area of Owners Lots. Total 1170m². Rates for Sydney NSW. No. of lots = 8 villas type of scheme. 2. Common Areas Contents requiring work, say 10% of Building Sum worked out by Registered Quantity Surveyor who ought to be the Required Valuer.			$2,608,420 $260,842	$2,608,420 $260,842
Progressive Total (PT-1)			$2,869,262	$2,869,262
Initial valuation escalation period: Valuation Report Date to Damage Policy Expiration Date period 31/05/2017–04/04/2019—based on time relative to the BPI over that period of days applicable and estimated 5% pa.-formula: 5 x 365 + (x) divided by 365 - (X=no of days > 365 over the period =428-365=63/365=0.17=5.17% over that period.	428	5.17%	$148,341	$148,341

Progressive Total (PT-2)			$3,017,603	$3,017,603
Demolition and site clean-up: say 5% x (PT-2)		5%	$150,880	$150,880
Progressive Total (PT-3)			$3,168,483	$3,168,483
Example Valuation 1: Professional Fees and Charges, say 10%		10%	$316,848	nil
Progressive Total 4 (PT-4)			$3,485,331	$3,168,483
Final valuation escalation period: BPI increase over the whole reinstatement period is 2 yrs. From Damage Policy Expiration Date 04/04/2019–04/04/2021—104 weeks under SSMR NSW 2016 - Reg.39—estimated 5% pa. Based on CoreLogic's BPI then rates for Sydney residential.	730	10%	$348,533	$316,848
Progressive Total 5 (PT-5) before GST			$3,833,864	$3,485,331
Plus GST		10%	$383,386	
Progressive total (PT-5) BSI PAA (GST Inclusive) = to the Minimum Replacement Value BSI Value as per SSMR NSW Reg. 39 Valuation 1.			**$4,217,250**	**$3,485,331**
Example Valuation 2: Increased Architect Fees and Charges, say 10% **after** final escalation but **before** Catastrophe loading showing an increase in its value.		10%	nil	$348,533
Progressive Total				$3,833,864
Catastrophe estimated costs BSI Value becomes the BSI FAA Value		+30%	nil	$4,984,023
Plus GST		10%	nil	$498,402
Progressive total				$5,482,426
(PT-5) BSI (PAA) as% of Catastrophe Cost (GST Inclusive) PAA divided by FAA is => 80% of catastrophe estimated cost **In Valuation 1 and 2: $4,217,250 / $5,482,426 = 76.92%** The 80% rule is unworkable for buildings				
SAFER TOTAL shows minimum RV as opposed to full costs BSI Value and location of Fees increases the BSI Value which is then based on *fuller but not yet on full costs,* as shown in Table 4.3				$5,482,426 Safer value

Table 4.2 shows my unique method to depict Architect Fees and Charges. The report date should be the same date as the site inspection date shown here as 31/05/2017; Damage policy commencement date: 04/04/2018; Damage policy expiration date: 04/04/2019. Percentage figures shown for clarity. Valuation 1 column shows Architect Fees and Charges based on minimum replacement value only while Valuation 2 allows for increased provision of Architect Fees and Charges based on *fuller but not yet on full costs,* as shown in Table 4.3

In Table 4.2, the valuation is calculated under SSMR NSW 2016 Reg. 39 that describes insurance for *at least the minimum replacement value immediately prior to the Event* but shows the difference in value when increased for catastrophe full costs value.

I term this the usual *minimum replacement value* BSI Value, which is about 30% below the estimated *catastrophe's* full costs BSI Value. The higher value might cover the costs and expenses incurred due to catastrophes in any type of low-rise building, provided the second escalation period factor remains at 104 weeks.

The duration of the insurance coverage and the projected period for costing the policy are subject to the impact of fiscal inflation, resulting in an increase in expenses (as measured by the Consumer Price Index [CPI]/Building Price Index [BPI]). It is important to take into consideration the possibility of a supply shortage. These values rise. The rate of the BPI consistently surpasses that of the CPI. The frequency of their decline is exceedingly rare.

Both the CPI and the BPI costs apply to strata schemes. These costs are allocated to the Administrative Fund, which manages present operational expenses and provisions for general repairs and maintenance. The Capital Works Fund covers estimated expenses for building works related to the building common area and common areas contents requiring maintenance.

During and after the pandemic period, rates have been inconsistent, and rental values have surpassed the typical annual CPI increases, leading to a significant impact on insurance values.

Currently in Australia, there is a severe scarcity of rental properties. This will exert a substantial impact on your BSI Value with minimum replacement value, given that expenses for temporary accommodation will be influenced by this scarcity, leading to significant gap costs.

There is no renter's protection for this occurrence. You must check your insurance policy annually for comparative market rental prices in your local area/s to keep your insurance BSI Value viable.

- Was this calculation factored in by the Productivity Commission when it repealed the Valuers Act 2003, to cut costs, assuming that insurance was a straightforward calculation of expenses? As with any endeavor, the key lies in understanding the process, which entails training, skills, experience, and adherence to professional registration regulations.

Underinsurance, defined as insuring only the minimum building replacement value, can cause the following gap costs:

- Demolition and Debris Removal costs
- Architect Fees and Charges
- escalated building costs due to demand
- loss of rent in terms of the rental contract
- temporary accommodation costs shortfall for at least 104 weeks for low-rise
- temporary accommodation costs shortfall for at least 208 weeks for high-rise
- planned statutory cost items required for a rebuild.

You still must afford ongoing property rates and taxes, management fees and charges and out-of-home living expenses until you can resume occupancy of your rebuilt home.

I defy anyone telling me how they define or enumerate being over insured—are they a clairvoyant?

Be aware that there are some Strata Managers who encourage owners to accept a lesser valuation on renewal and the resultant lower premium price. I have experienced this. The unfortunate incident led me to carry out research and present this work.

Once again, to assess underinsurance with the minimum replacement value chosen, if the specified amount for comparable housing for typically 104 weeks is not equal to or greater than 15% of the selected BSI Value, you are likely underinsured.

Looking at Table 4.1, the 15% value of the minimum replacement value $483,447 is $72,517.

The comparative value you would have needed in 2018 was about $700 per week for rental accommodation (the then asking price in my area for my type of home). So, take the minimum value $700 x 104 = $72,800. You could, for good measure, increase this value by 10% (or the current inflation rental rate for the forward estimates as referenced by CoreLogic or other authoritive body such as PropTrack, to cover the inflation CPI rental rate over the forward period for a minimum of 2 years for low-rise and a minimum of 4 years for high-rise structures.) That would now show a value of $80,080. Pitting that against the minimum Replacement Value, the amount will be: $80,080 divided by 15% = $533,867.

Your minimum insurance value was $483,447, meaning a potential shortfall for accommodation value of $50,420.

Can you see now that the minimum Replacement Value would not support or sustain the costs for accommodation during the planned period? You are way underinsured with minimum replacement value only. The minimum asking price may not be available in your area, so cost may further increase for a different size home or a home in another area unsuitable for your lifestyle.

In Table 4.2, the comparative value for loss of rent/temporary accommodation value from the typical low-rise strata residential policy would be 15% of $4,217,250 = $632,588

Taking the minimum value asking price for similar accommodation as $700 per week, the total minimum current market rental value needed for 8 villas for 104 weeks would amount to $700 x 104 x 8 = $582,400

When comparing it to the suggested catastrophe full costs value in Column Valuation 2, the BSI Value amounts to $5,482,426.00.

The identical calculation (15% of $5,482,426) would cause an increase in the accommodation value to $822,364, significantly surpassing the minimum market rental price ($582,400). You are in a secure state. Rental costs may experience a significant increase before you incur accommodation gap expenses.

But, in a rebuild scenario, Architect Fees and Charges would be under-provided for as the value for Fees is based on the minimum Replacement Value only and not on full costs value.

Table 4.3 applies the full costs appraisal for Architect Fees and Charges—the safer valuation method to minimize gap costs.

Table 4.3 A Potential High-rise 100% Catastrophe Estimated Full Costs BSI Value

Description: My innovative method to provide	Days	%	Valuation 1 Minimum RV BSI Value	Valuation 2 Catastrophe Full Costs BSI Value
1. Total building gross area of Owners Lots. Total 1170m². Rates for Sydney NSW. No. of lots = 8 villas type of scheme. 2. Common Areas Contents requiring work, say 10% of Building Sum worked out by Registered Quantity Surveyor.			$2,608,420 $260,842	$2,608,420 $260,842
Progressive Total (PT-1)			$2,869,262	$2,869,262
Initial valuation escalation period: Valuation Report Date to Damage Policy Expiration Date 31/05/2017-04/04/2019— based on time relative to the BPI over that period of days applicable and estimated 5% pa. —formula: 5 x 365 + (x) divided by 365 - (X=no of days > 365 over the period =428-365=63/365=0.17=5.17% over that period.	428	5.17%	$148,341	$148,341
Progressive Total (PT-2)			$3,017,603	$3,017,603
Demolition and site clean-up: say 5% x (PT-2)		5%	$150,880	$150,880

Progressive Total (PT-3)			$3,168,483	$3,168,483
Example Valuation 1: Professional Fees and Charges, say 10% BEFORE CATASTROPHE LOADING Fees Value 1		10%	$316,848	nil
Progressive Total 4 (PT-4)			$3,485,331	$3,168,483
Final valuation escalation period: BPI increase over the whole reinstatement period is 4 yrs. (1460 days) **From** Damage Policy Expiration Date—estimated 5% pa. Based on CoreLogic's BPI, the then rates for Sydney residential housing.	1460	+20%	$4,182,397	$3,802,180
Add GST		10%	$383,386	$348,533
Progressive total 5 (PT-5)			$4,600,637	$4,182,398
Progressive total (PT-5) BSI Preliminary Adoption Amount (PAA) (GST Inclusive) = to the min. BSI Value as per SSMR NSW 2016 Reg. 39			$4,600,637	
100% Catastrophe estimated full costs BSI Value (GST Inclusive) becomes the BSI Final Adoption Amount (FAA) shown below.		+30%	nil	$5,437,117
Example Valuation 2: Increased Professional Fees and Charges, say 10% AFTER CATASTROPHE LOADING Fees Value 2		10%	nil	$543,712
Progressive Total				$5,980,829
Add GST		10%	nil	$598,083
Progressive Total FAA Value after catastrophe 30% + Fees on full costs				$6,578,912
(PT-5) BSI (PAA) as% of Catastrophe Cost (GST Inclusive) PAA divided by FAA is => 80% of catastrophe estimated cost In Valuation 1: Min. RV divided by BSI Value $4,600,637 / $6,578,912 = 69.93% The 80% rule is unworkable for buildings.				
SAFEST TOTAL 100% POTENTIAL INSURANCE PAYOUT			$4,600,637 Traditional Min. RV	$6,578,912 Innovative Safer Value

Table 4.3 shows the unique method for calculating Architect Fees and Charges. The report date should be the same date as the site inspection date shown here as 31/05/2017; Damage policy commencement date: 04/04/2018; Damage policy expiration date: 04/04/2019. Percentage figures shown for clarity. Table 4.3 exhibits a distinction from Table 4.2 in terms of Valuation 2, where Architect Fees and Charges are determined based on estimated full costs after the application of catastrophe loading, as opposed to before it is applied.

Table 4.3. This cover is for *extended* estimated full extra costs and is most useful for high-rise complexes. The building valuation escalation period is increased to *at least* 208 weeks to allow for a greater period for replacement to occur, and includes:

Extended escalation provision for accommodation costing for at least 208 weeks but does not include additional local council statutory planned building-related costing, which influences the rebuild estimated cost.

Please consult Table 4.4 for including local council statutory planned building-related code compliance costing. Alternatively, you may choose to adapt Table 4.3 to incorporate it for insurance valuation purposes of older type buildings.

Table 4.4 A Potential High-rise 100% Catastrophe Estimated Full Costs BSI Value Using Rental Values in forming the BSI Value

Description: The BSI Value is determined through an original and unorthodox approach using rental values and is useful for providing individual rental values for the division of proportional costs.	Days	%	Full Valuation
1. The X space tenancy component $ Rental Value is inputted. 2. The Y space tenancy components/s $ Rental Value/s are added. The gross building areas and common areas contents requiring work value are included in the rental value.			= $ = $
Progressive Total			$
Initial escalation period 1: Valuation Report Date to Damage Policy Expiration Date period 31/05/2017-04/04/2019—based on time relative to the Building Price Index (BPI) over that period of days applicable and estimated 5% pa. –formula: 5% + (x) divided by 365 - (X=no of days > 365 over the period =428-365=63/365=0.17 +5 =5.17%	428	+5.17%	Total $ value of PT-1 + 5.17% = $
Progressive Total (PT-1)			$ Summation
Demolition and site clean-up: say 5% of PT-1		+5%	$
Progressive Total (PT-2)			$ Summation
4. The Z code compliance costing is now added.			$

Progressive Total (PT-3)			$ Summation
Final escalation period 2: BPI increase over the whole reinstatement period is at least 208 weeks, from Damage Policy Expiration Date 04/04/2021—estimated 5% pa. (5% + (x) divided by 365 when (X=no of days > 365 over the period thus: 1460-365=1095/365=3 +5 = 8%)	1460	+8%	Add escalation to PT-3
Progressive Total (PT-4)			$ Summation
5. Add catastrophe loading (for escalated building costs)		+15%	
Progressive Total (PT-5)			$ Summation
6. Architect Fees and Charges, say 10% (could be greater)		+10%	**$ of PT-5 x 10%**
Progressive Total (PT-6)			**$** Summation
General Sales Tax (GST) currently 10%		+10%	**$ of PT-6 + 10%**
Progressive total (PT-7) FAA Value = super-charged catastrophe full costs BSI Value			$ Summation

Note: Architect Fees and Charges are inputted after the catastrophe loading lower down in the table to gain maximum escalation factor, thus increasing the Value for Architect Fees and Charges value saving gap costs.

In Table 4.4, the BSI Value is determined through an original and unorthodox approach using rental values. The method shown is also useful for determining the division of proportional costs for repairs and maintenance costs and, thus, also for the proportional payment value for splitting the insurance premium value between the various building space tenancy components and all other administrative costs.

Shown by the x and y components in the hypothetical building composition exemplar above, the rental value is directly relatable to the BSI Value as evidenced by the percentage breakdown (the 15% value)—which, incidentally, is also the accommodation value for 208 weeks.

This equation resolves and makes simpler the NSW Strata Act Sec. 162 (2) Insurance premiums where the strata scheme is for part only of building:

The premium for a damage policy is to be paid by the owners corporation or other person according to the proportion that the replacement value of the part (or parts) of the building subject to the strata scheme or held in fee simple by the other person bears to the replacement value of the whole building.

It should be emphasized that the assessment of each lot's responsibility for payment of the damage policy premium by the owners corporation does not involve the use of unequal Lot Entitlements.

In Table 4.4, weekly rental values are used, as they result in a more accurate calculation.

Thus, the total aggregate of the ***annual*** *median weekly rental values* of **all strata lots** multiplied by at least 208 weeks (or other perceived greater period estimated required to replace the building) will provide the total rental value for the strata lots.

This total rental value can provide for:

- a comparative value for the sharing of costs for repairs and maintenance, and
- importantly, if that total rental value is divided by 15%, it will provide a value equivalent to the BSI Value to be input into the Valuation Table and is also the accommodation value.

That means where "x" forms a strata lot component, the calculation is:

"x" is the aggregate total value of all lots' average annual rental value.

Thus:

- Average rental value x 52 x 208 weeks (minimum period for high-rise rebuild or greater period perceived required) divided by 15% equals the aggregate total BSI Value for the strata residential component of the building.

Market rental values can be obtained from the local real estate agent. These values are based on the whole of the building's features and attributes of common areas requiring work. The median rental value is the average of the lowest and highest lot rental values. Insurance is an estimation of costs, and this also simplifies the sharing of costs on a fairer basis.

- To calculate the aggregate total of the other volumetric space component/s of the building, the *actual annual weekly rental value/s* of the component/s are multiplied by at least 208 weeks (or other perceived greater period, like the above equation).

That means the *actual weekly rent value* multiplied by 52 multiplied by at least 208 weeks and divided by 15% equals the aggregate total/s BSI Value for the volumetric component/s of the building. If there is more than one, a similar calculation should be done for the other volumetric components.

- Those combined aggregate totals for the residential and volumetric components and the statutory costing value z (x + all the y's + z) form the *super-charged catastrophe estimated full costs BSI Value*. The z costing is the code compliance short list compiled by the professional team.

The result is that when the above aggregate total rental values are input into the table in Table 4.4, they form the base BSI Value—the PAA Value.

The Insurance Percentage Schedule Value for the line items pertaining to catastrophe and loss of rent/temporary accommodation is based on the BSI Value (Building value) mentioned in the Building Valuation Schedule of Offer, which is subsequently augmented by the final selected increased BSI Value, also referred to as the FAA Value.

> To digress slightly, for readers situated globally, please take note. The utilization of unequal Lot Entitlements for proportional cost division and voting rights in Strata should be avoided. The method of determining shared expenses in British Columbia, Canada's Strata Titles Act and

Regulations—originally modeled after the NSW Strata Act and Regulations—relies on the aggregation of habitable areas. I consider that method unsafe.

The evaluation of building insurance is determined by the gross area of the buildings, along with the contents of common areas that require repair and maintenance. The innovative approach I use mirrors the association between the market rental values, the characteristics and amenities of the building, and the insurance BSI value, which has a direct correlation to the rental values. Thus, the BSI Value is calculated by considering the current market values.

The allocation of repair and maintenance costs ought to be determined by computing the proportional percentage value of the market rental proportional percentage values of the total building area components.

Thus, for example, the proportional percentage value for the x component, for cost sharing, would be:

$$\% \text{ value for } x = \frac{x}{Y1 + Y2} \text{ multiplied by } 100$$

The fairest method for cost-sharing is to use the Market Rental Value, which is directly linked to the value of insurance. When the focus is on establishing insurance value that is in line with market rental values, it becomes possible to address all expenses associated with repairs and maintenance for the building complex based on their proportionate percentage values.

The Formulation of the Super-charged Value

To help you understand the formulation for the high-rise **super-charged catastrophe estimated full costs BSI Value,** an exemplar is shown below.

The typical mixed-use high-rise building may comprise various parts or components, such as residential, hotel, and commercial shopping areas, for example. A hypothetical situation is shown below in a building scheme composition example.

Common building features and services are considered when assessing rental values.

Hypothetical Building Scheme Composition Example

"x" = Residential strata scheme component is covered by the aggregate of the annual **median** weekly lot rental values.
"y1" = Hotel volumetric component is covered by the actual annual aggregate weekly rental value.
"y2" = Commercial shopping area is covered by the actual annual aggregate weekly rental value, to simplify the estimated costing.

It is important to note that the only required schedule is the brief list of code compliance, as other schedules, such as the disturbing unequal lot entitlement schedule that displays quantities of any kind, are unnecessary. I do not encourage the utilization of such schedules as they are redundant and do not correspond to the above fairer correlation of values.

Now, x = aggregate for all strata residential lots costed as above.

y1 and y2 = aggregate for all volumetric lots costed as above.

Let z denote the sum of the short list of building components necessary for code compliance in a reconstruction. The building's professional team must present the gross building area/areas and common areas content that require work to the Registered Quantity Surveyor for costing.

A simplified short list for code compliance costing may include:

- Sustainability/climate change—switch out of electrical generation system to full electric.
- Accessibility design issues of entry/egress and health requirements for restrooms and toilets.

- Modern fire prevention systems, including pressurized stairs areas.
- Security features covering common areas.
- Increased parking requirements.
- Switch-out of faulty building materials, cladding if still required to be attended to.

z becomes the total of the Registered Quantity Surveyor calculation for statutory compliance.

$x + y1 + y2 + z$ = base super-charged value to which must be added the initial and final escalation period values, estimated demolition cost, catastrophe loading, Architect Fees and Charges and general sales tax on the whole aggregated value as shown in Table 4.4.

That total FAA Value will now = the **high-rise super-charged catastrophe estimated full costs BSI Value.**

Below is a UK-based building cost calculator for a replacement valuation method. [9]

BCIS Rebuilding Cost Guidance

> The Building Cost Information Service (BCIS) produces a range of detailed guidance on the cost of rebuilding houses and flats. The *Association of British Insurers (ABI)* has commissioned BCIS to provide general guidance to help you check the adequacy of your sum insured.
>
> This site provides general guidance on the rebuilding cost of houses and some types of flats to the general public. If you require the rebuilding cost for commercial purposes, either as a surveyor, part of the insurance industry or to manage a group of properties then you should be using one of the

---

9   https://calculator.bcis.co.uk/

> BCIS subscription services. You can find details of services for the insurance industry at <u>https://bcis.co.uk/products/insurance</u> and services for the surveying profession at <u>https://bcis.co.uk/products/real-estate/residential-property</u>.
>
> You need to register before using this calculator. As a part of the registration process you must accept the <u>terms and conditions of use</u>. Once registered, you will be able to use the calculator four times in any 12-month period. Please refer to the notes on this site, which provide important information on your rebuilding cost.

The notes state to use the guide to get a rough idea for the rebuild cost so you don't end up paying any shortfall!

It also says:

> You only need to insure your house for its rebuild cost. Please note that if you are a member of the public looking for an insurance reinstatement cost for your home, visit the **<u>House rebuilding cost calculator</u>**, which is a free service. The information is that the calculator is intended for checking sums insured and is no substitute for professional advice and judgment, particularly where a property has any unusual features or is outside the range of properties described for the use of the calculator, and if the rebuilding cost from the calculator is markedly different from your current sum insured, contact your insurance company, broker, or a local chartered surveyor.

I stress you should use none of these tools but should get professional information from a Registered Quantity Surveyor. The costing formulation should be like the ones shown in the Valuation Tables shown above, where the make-up of costs method is transparent. Armed with that information, you can make up your own mind as to the BSI Value you would be comfortable with.

Note: The *surveying profession* mentioned by BCIS above is apparently those members of the RICS for England or Scotland, respectively.

In the US, there is also a range of property insurance policies.

In his book—*The Property Insurance B.I.B.L.E.*, author Abraham Kevin Spann says:

- *Tenants should protect their current assets with an affordable Renters Insurance policy.*
- *Shareholders and Co-operatives should protect their belongings with a Co-op or Condo Insurance policy.*
- *Homeowners policies include coverage to replace the Dwelling and any other structures on the property.*
- *Personal property is protected at 50% to 70% of the replacement cost of the dwelling coverage amount.*
- *Landlords should protect their property with a DP-3 policy. DP-3 policies include loss of rental income.*
- *Homes that are vacant for over thirty days need a Vacant Insurance policy.*
- *Water is the most common cause of property damage, and the average claim is valued at $5,000.*
- *Make sure you get the maximum amount of water backup coverage offered by your carrier.*
- *Flood Insurance and Mortgage Protection Life Insurance are never included in a standard home insurance policy.*
- *A Personal Umbrella policy (PUP) is an excess liability policy to protect clients from unforeseen accidents, lawsuits, catastrophes, and natural disasters.*
- *The key coverages are the same for all carriers. There's coverage A - the dwelling coverage to repair or replace your home. Coverage*

> B of Other structures Protection. This covers any additional structures on your property, such as a detached garage, shed, gazebo, etc. Personal Property is protected under Coverage C. It is generally set to a formula of 70% of the dwelling coverage.

- *Additional Living Expenses (ALE) or Loss of Use is the coverage that will pay to put you and your family in a hotel if your home can't be occupied due to a covered loss.*
- *Coverage E is the Comprehensive Personal Liability coverage on a home insurance policy.*
- *Under Coverage C, clarify if you are covered for Full Replacement Cost or an Actual Cash Value.*

The important thing to note is that Spann failed to mention that you will need to know how to select the correct Sum Insured Value—the BSI Value—for whatever type of property you are associated with. Nothing in his book covers this aspect!

Co-insurance

Some insurance companies assert their policies do not have co-insured clauses. Presumably that refers to the 80% Average Provision Rule.

It is imperative to note that to avail the additional benefits of 15% extra to the BSI Value for catastrophe schedule value and all other additional benefits, the BSI Value must be greater than 80% of the Replacement Value immediately prior to the Event as per the Longitude Strata Residential Building Insurance Policy. It is also important to note that additional benefits would not be provided in the absence of a *declared catastrophe* by a third-party authority announcement, as per an additional conditional and limitational clause.

The policy in question, or any other policy, does not specify the method of value calculation, and there is no legal obligation in NSW or elsewhere to include the Building Insurance Valuation Report in the insurance contract documents to clarify the values for minimum value and full costs value.

In cases such as Longitude, the values for both *catastrophe and loss of rent/temporary accommodation* are mentioned under the Catastrophe clause.

Cautionary notes regarding the sums insured as Scheduled Additional Benefits or extra costs, meaning:

- Catastrophe Schedule Sum Insured Value
- Loss of Rent/Temporary Accommodation Schedule Sum Insured Value.

Operationalization of these Scheduled Additional Benefits or extra costs **is not automatic** but subject to conditions and limitations described differently in each policy you may select. Refer to Chapter 3, Fig. 3.2 for some comparison clues.

In the UK, why have Condominiums or Commonholds, as they are called, not taken off?

Referring to the Blog of the CAI[10]

> *Condominiums have taken off in Europe too, especially in France and Germany. However, one country remains a laggard in this trend: The United Kingdom.*
>
> *Despite* legislation *introduced in 2004 to jump-start condominiums— or commonholds as they are referred in the U.K—*less than 20 *have been developed.*
> *The commonhold system was introduced to phase out the most popular form of housing in the UK: leasehold. In a*

---

10 https://blog.caionline.org why-are-common-interest-communities-so-uncommon-in-the-u-k/

leasehold arrangement, the buyer rents a flat from the freeholder, or landlord, for a specified number of years. The freeholder is responsible for managing and maintaining the common areas of the building, such as hallways, roofs, and facades. The lease is typically long-term—often as many as 120 years—but begins to decrease in value as the lease nears its end. Many individuals have taken issue with the leasehold system. Complaints range from burdensome fees imposed by landlords to the costliness of extending a lease and the fundamental nature of a leasehold as a wasting asset.

With all the complaints surrounding leaseholds, one might wonder why there's a lack of enthusiasm for commonholds? In theory, self-management of commonholds removes conflict with the landlord, and ownership alleviates the ticking time bomb worry of a lease. The Law Commission, *an entity responsible for reforming laws in the UK, has a few ideas as to why commonholds remain so sparse.*

Some potential issues affect homeowners. When changing from a leasehold to a commonhold, the law requires unanimous consent from every inhabitant 21 years or older, the freeholder, and every lender with a mortgage.

Naturally, getting this many people informed, let alone on board with such a big change, is difficult. In addition, the **commonhold association**, *the UK equivalent of a* **community association board**, *is a company under the current law.*

As such, leaseholders could face criminal penalties for violating the law. This standard is much too risky for any homeowner.

Regulations also might be too stringent in some areas and overly flexible in others. For example, maintenance obligations are unchangeable regardless of age and price of the building, but on the other hand, fire insurance is the only

<u>type of insurance</u> *buildings are required to have, whereas other types of buildings require flooding and theft insurance.*

Overall, commonhold's failure to launch might simply be due to lack of a financial incentive for developers and a gap in public awareness over this type of housing. These types of large-scale transitions can be difficult and require public backing. However, the UK's housing reform endeavors are an admirable effort to jump-start conversation between potential homebuyers, legislators, commonhold owners, and developers.

Commentary on the above legislative provisions

Despite efforts to establish and advance commonholds, the underlying issue is failing to adhere to historical evidence, whereby strata entities in Australia are governed by their respective State/Territory Strata Titles Act, rather than being subject to the Corporations Act. This is without delving into the intricacies of GST treatment.

The collective ownership of the project by the community is established, resulting in a gradual increase in the value of both the property and individual lots in line with market rates, with no time restriction on ownership. The determination of the Administrative and Capital Works budgets lies with the Owners' Corporation. Lot Owners have the freedom to sell their individual lots with no obligations.

UK Law Commission: Commonhold call for evidence. [11]

Commonhold costs

Homeowners will be required to contribute towards the costs of maintaining and managing the commonhold (for example, the cost of repairing the roof or paying a caretaker).

---

11   https://s3-eu-west-2.amazonaws.com/lawcom-prod-storage-11jsxou24uy7q/uploads/2018/02/Commonhold-Call-For-Evidence.pdf

The share to be paid by each homeowner is set out in each commonhold's community statement.

This share will be the same regardless of what the cost relates to. We have been told that this is not flexible enough and that it should be possible to split costs in a way that better reflects the actual use of services and facilities.

Example:

There is a commonhold building with a shop on the ground floor, one flat taking up the entire first floor and two flats sharing the second floor. When the commonhold was set up, it was decided that the first floor flat and shop owners should pay slightly more than the other units. The commonhold community statement therefore allocates the commonhold expenses in the following way:

- *Shop and Flat 1: 30% each of the commonhold costs.*
- *Flats 2 and 3: 20% each of the commonhold costs.*

Figure 1: This allocation means that when the roof of the building needs repairing, the shop and first floor flat owners will be required to pay 30% each of the cost, whilst the owners of flats 2 and 3 will pay 20% each.

Outside the building there is a small car park with 10 spaces. Each flat has one allocated parking space, and the remaining seven spaces are allocated to the shop.

Figure 2: Even though the shop has seven spaces (70% of the car park) and the flat owners only have one each (10% each), the cost of maintaining the car park must be shared in the same way as the cost of repairing the roof. The shop and first floor flat owners both pay 30% of the cost and flats 2 and 3 will pay 20% each. It has been argued that there should be flexibility to split the costs in a way that better reflects actual usage – in this case, so that the shop owner pays 70% of the cost of maintaining the car park, with the owners of flats 1, 2 and 3 each contributing 10%.

We have been told that one way to add flexibility would be to permit the creation of "layers" within a commonhold. This could involve each component part of a mixed-use development having its own commonhold association which would deal with issues specific to that part. For instance, there could be one commonhold association to manage the residential element of the development and another to manage the commercial element. There would then be an overarching "umbrella commonhold" which would cover the entire development and address issues common to the whole development.

Example: A private estate is built with the following:

(A) a large block containing 20 residential flats

(B) 20 detached houses

(C) a restaurant and a shop; and

(D) a driveway and gardens shared between all the properties.

Commonhold could be used for this development. Under the current law there would be just one commonhold association, made up of the residential flat owners, the shop and restaurant owners, and the owners of the houses. All the costs would be shared between all the owners, and all the owners would be able to vote on all matters. This would be the case even if the matter in question only related to one group of owners (for example, deciding what color to paint the staircases in the block of flats).

It might be more desirable to be able to create a "layered scheme" in the following way.

> *(1) An "umbrella" commonhold association would be set up, which would deal with matters affecting all owners, such as the upkeep of the road and shared gardens.*
>
> *(2) Three sub-commonholds could then be created:*
>
>> *(a)   one made up of all the house owners, dealing with issues relating only to the houses.*
>>
>> *(b)   one made up of all the residential flat owners; and*
>>
>> *(c)   one made up of the commercial owners.*
>
> *This would create a commonhold structure.*
>
> *In addition, we have been told that more flexibility is required in both the way costs can be allocated and in the commonhold community statement. These concerns have already been referred to above in our discussion of issues making commonhold unattractive to homeowners. However, these are also issues which might deter developers from choosing commonhold over leasehold. In particular, the community statement has been criticized for not catering to the needs of particularly large, or particularly small, developments.*

Commentary on the above

Refer to Table 4.4 to see how costs for repairs and maintenance costs are derived based on rental values of the component space tenancy parts of the building.

The fundamental issue making commonhold unattractive to developers is that, first, the law needs to be changed to separate commonhold from the general corporations' law and, second, management costs need to be structured differently and shared across the board.

> *Unsatisfactory security for mortgage lenders. The UK Finance Mortgage Lenders' Handbook (which provides guidance for conveyancers acting for mortgage lenders) indicates that*

around 70% of the institutions listed will not lend on a commonhold unit. Those that will not lend include major lenders such as Santander and the Royal Bank of Scotland. We have been told that the reluctance to lend on commonhold may be partly due to a lack of certainty over what happens to lenders' security if the commonhold ends, for instance, in insolvency. We would like to find out whether this is a concern in practice and whether there may be other reasons commonhold is unacceptable to most lenders.

The above statement warrants a commentary.

The present commonhold structure prohibits a proprietor from owning a lot, which implies that there is no property to leverage a mortgage against. It is uncertain what will happen to lenders' security in the event of commonhold termination, such as during insolvency. In addition, the current building insurance requirements are inadequate since they cannot offer complete protection to the property against a variety of environmental incidents. This is especially clear in Australia, where building insurance covers more than just fire, and the notion of at least the value of replacement value, for the entire complex, is paramount.

Chapter Five

NON-STRATA GENERAL HOME INSURANCE POLICIES

Quoted text is presented in italics and indented.

 ## 5.1 GENERAL COMMENT AND KEY POINTS

- In the US, a homeowner's policy includes contents in the same policy. Values for contents are typically 50% to 70% of the BSI Value. Tangible articles need to have an exact replacement value stated so that the replacement value after an Event can be assessed against the purchase price. The 80% Average Provision Rule for tangible assets could apply where a Cash Value instead of the Replacement Value may apply.

- It is customary in Australia also, for providers to offer a combination of General Home insurance and Contents insurance, resulting in perplexity among customers due to non-standardized terms, conditions, and restrictions.

- This publication asserts that the general phraseology employed in home insurance policies is insufficient and non-standardized in terms of payout specifications.

- The absence of related rental contract values for loss of rent cost and standard percentage values for temporary accommodation expense, if you cannot live in your home or if you cannot lease your home, is the reason behind this.

- If your insurance coverage falls short of covering your loss, the home policy may specify an additional safety net of up to 25% besides your BSI Value, to cover the gap costs of repairing, rebuilding, or replacing your property and/or belongings.

- All costs are only considered valid after they have been spent. There will be zero gap cover payment in the event of a total loss declaration.
- Additional expenses, where applicable, are inconsistent. Loss of rent costs are incorrectly accounted for, and accommodation expenses are inadequately accounted for and usually below the value that you would need, resulting in large gap costs.
- My recommendation is to avoid concurrent purchase of both building and contents worded in the same insurance policy document, given that the joint policies espouse both the indemnity value and the replacement value philosophies, which may cause confusion and inaccuracy when assessing the worth of tangible and intangible assets.
- The insurer's usual role does not involve rebuilding the structure but repairing it. The decision to rebuild is that of the owner/s.
- The policyholder trusts that the Valuation Schedule Offer, or a similar safety net provided in home insurance policies, *will apply and be guaranteed* when opting for a contract offer. However, they may later realize that the additional benefits for costs arising should have been planned into the BSI Value at the time the BSI Value was selected.
- This means your BSI Value should have been upped to at least cover the price of temporary housing for at least 104 weeks after the policy runs out. You could, in addition, up it further to account for the escalation in building costs due to supply. That means increasing the base minimum replacement value by 30%. High-rise structures require further upping, as referenced in Chapter 4, Table 4.4.
- Typically, the compensation amount for total loss value is based solely on the minimum replacement value determined by the BSI Value. This may be the case with home insurance or, even worse, with strata building insurance where a lesser depreciated Indemnity Value may be offered in settlement.
- This can lead to a reduction in the Sum Insured, which is changed by a loss adjuster or valuer chosen by the insurer. The adjusted value is compared to the value of the building when it was first constructed. NSW strata law avails this practice in its "Limitation of Value" clause!

- To exacerbate the situation, the Insurance Contact Act 1984 (Commonwealth) Sec. 48 applies in Australia. Under Clause 48, the third-party beneficiary clause, payment will be made to a financier or bank to settle any outstanding loan, regardless of whether the beneficiary is named in the insurance contract and regardless of your preferences.
- It is plausible that a claimant who is a third-party beneficiary could completely exhaust the insurance value, leaving the insured with no residual value from the insurance policy that they had purchased to safeguard their family. I am advocating for a change in this law.
- I also advocate for **general home insurance** to be inclusive with the NSW Strata Schemes Act and Regulations and Law, specifically amended to include the additional benefits to be paid besides the BSI Value with destruction, catastrophe, total loss, and constructive total loss.
- It is pointless for lawyers to write to newspapers to complain about the denial culture of insurance policies. Lawyers who oversee the Commonwealth and State laws have the power to make the changes advocated for. Until that occurs, the status quo will not be changed, and justice, fairness, and transparency will not be served.

For **General Home Underinsurance**, refer to the ICA Report. [12]

Extracts from this report:

> *While it is difficult to measure the level of underinsurance in Australia, insurers know that this is a real and significant issue that can affect policyholders' ability to get back on their feet after an unforeseen event.*
>
> *Sometimes, insurers have no option but to offer a cash payment rather than reinstate what has been damaged or destroyed because the level of insurance the policyholder has*

---

12   https://insurancecouncil.com.au/wp-content/uploads/2021/09/ICA008_CatastropheReport_6.5_FA1_online.pdf

taken out will not cover the cost of a repair or rebuild. This leaves the policyholder to make up the difference, or sometimes walking away from a property they cannot afford to rebuild.

Insurers provide tools such as online calculators to help estimate the sum insured, but the customer may decide to insure at a lower sum as self-insurance or may not accurately estimate the replacement value of their property.

Underinsurance is also driven by stamp duty on insurance, a retrograde revenue measure that many inquiries and reviews have found leads to household underinsurance or non-insurance. Government taxes and charges can range from 20 to 40 percent on top of the cost of the premium, depending on the state or territory.

While the ICA Board catastrophe code declaration may assist the insured claimants on the ground by standing up resources to respond to claimants affected by an event, the declaration *should not* be written into an insurance policy as a definition of catastrophe, triggering when the Additional Benefits, extra costs, or safety net apply. Such a third-party decision may represent a conflict of interest.

The Insurance Contract Act 1984 (Commonwealth) states that a damage policy is between the insurer and insured.

The Table 4.3 cost valuation formulation framework, which provides for catastrophe full costs valuation, should be the same for either strata or general home insurance purposes, and calculators should not be used, as they are inaccurate. Instead, the services of a Registered Quantity Surveyor should only be used for insurance valuations where an Owners' Corporation has three lots or more on one site and title.

For other properties, a registered member of the API, who is a Certified Practicing Valuer (CPV), could be used. The API is the only Australian valuation institute recognized by the International Valuation Standards Council (IVSC).

So much for the NSW Productivity Commission repealing the Valuers Act 2003 in March 2016.

Tax on insurance policies has nothing to do with the prospective insured's selection of the BSI Value, but the additional imposition of taxes on the value of insurance is, agreeably, a disincentive and *potentially harmful* for the prospective insured, where the consumer cannot take out insurance because of the additional taxation cost factor, including GST tax on top of the other taxes, making the product and the protection it offers more expensive and possibly unaffordable.

> *Statistics illustrate that the level of taxes imposed on insurance correlates to the rate of underinsurance and non-insurance. For example, because of its Emergency Services Levy, the (State imposed tax) on insurance in New South Wales is almost three times higher than in Victoria.*

> *Australian Bureau of Standards (ABS) data shows that 13 percent of households are uninsured in New South Wales, while in Victoria this rate is just seven percent.*

(Data also shows that 30% of all homeowners in Australia carry a mortgage.)

Does that mean because of stamp duty only or also because of extensive areas prone to bushfire and flooding? Both bushfire and flooding events result in the base cost of insurance being expensive or unobtainable. This is before additional tax costs (increasing the GST cost factor—tax on tax) are added. This is exactly where consumers should not be without building insurance to protect their assets and psychological wellbeing.

Tax on insurance has no community benefit and is therefore counterproductive and harmful. Governments are supposed to protect the community.

> The sixth ICA policy measure—Removing state taxes on insurance—is to be acted upon to better protect Australians from the impact of natural disasters and improve the recovery and rebuilding process when disaster strikes. This is hampered by state taxes and charges driving up the cost of premiums. The tax system should encourage, not hinder, insurance coverage. To improve [I say, to mitigate] levels of underinsurance, all states and territories should abolish stamp duty on insurance, and New South Wales and Tasmania should follow other states and abolish their Emergency and Fire Services Levies.

For a case example of underinsurance, the below commentary refers to p. 23 of the ICA Resilience Report ("The impact of underinsurance") referred to below.

> When a total loss is declared/considered by the insurer and insurers have no option but to offer a cash payment rather than reinstate what has been damaged or destroyed because of the level of insurance the policyholder has taken out will not cover the cost of a repair or rebuild.

That *cash payment* does not include any additional benefits, or a safety net, being added to the base BSI Value of the contract value. This is because the law affecting insurance does not protect those additional benefits in the policy and their respective valuation, as stated and shown in the Building Insurance Valuation Schedule of Offer or described as a safety net provision.

The accommodation value in non-strata policies should be standardized and statutorily payable besides the base BSI Value with *destruction, catastrophe, total loss, and constructive total loss.*

That is also why I advocate for the harmonization of strata and non-strata building insurance.

5.2   A Look at the NRMA House Building Insurance Policy PDS—called Home Insurance, effective date July 2021[13]

The PDS includes a supplementary PDS (SPDS), which applies to new policies effective from 15 July 2021 or for renewals with an effective date on or after 16 August 2021. An SPDS is issued after the initial release date.

> **Catastrophe** *means an event declared by the Insurance Council of Australia to be a Catastrophe—for example, fire, flood, earthquake, cyclone, severe storm, or hail, resulting in many insurance claims and involving multiple insurers.*

That is not the exact wording in the ICA Code.

> **Code** *means the General Insurance Code of Practice 2020.*

> **Extraordinary Catastrophe** *means a* **Catastrophe** *that is so significant or in magnitude or one that coincides with multiple other* **Catastrophes** *that the Board of the Insurance Council of Australia declares it to be extraordinary.*

So what? How does that relate to catastrophe insured values that should be payable?

---

[13]   https://www.nrma.com.au/sites/nrma/files/nrma/policy_booklets/home_pds_0219_nsw_act_tas.pdfhttps://www.nrma.com.au/sites/nrma/files/nrma/policy_booklets/home_pds_0721_nsw_act_tas.pdf
Current Version - Home insurance PDS July 2021
For policies that started on 15 July 2021 or were renewed from 16 August 2021.

Insured *means a person, company or entity holding, or seeking to hold, a general insurance product covered by this Code. It excludes a Third-Party Beneficiary—but refers to the below wording/definition for third-party beneficiary.*

Third Party Beneficiary *means a person, company or entity who is not insured but who is seeking to be, is specified to be, or is referred to as, a person to whom the benefit of the insurance cover extends. This Code must cover the relevant product. The person, company or entity may be specified by, or referred to by, name or otherwise.*

A Third-Party Beneficiary is NOT excluded from general insurance because of the Insurance Contract Act 1984 (Commonwealth) Sec. 48 (1).

*(1) A **third-party beneficiary** under a contract of general insurance has a right to recover from the insurer, under the contract, the amount of any loss suffered by the third-party beneficiary even though the third-party beneficiary is not a party to the contract.*

The above Act wording and the insurance policy wording are difficult to comprehend, as the Act refers to the words "under the contract" and "any loss suffered."

The inclusion of this provision in all three home insurance policies examined in this publication implies that the bank or financier will be reimbursed via a letter delineating the remaining loan balance. This occurrence may happen irrespective of the homeowner's ability to maintain payments, the homeowner's intention to continue loan servicing, and even if obtaining another loan is not feasible due to the circumstances.

Governing law and GST. *This contract is governed by the law of the Australian State or Territory that your home is in.*

What about Commonwealth contract laws, under which the Insurance Contract Act 1984 falls?

When you open the NRMA booklet, you are confronted with a complex array of different coverage options, including:

(a) Home

(b) Home Plus

(c) Building Insurance, which covers your home, either Home (standard) or Home Plus (highest level of cover)

(d) Contents Insurance covers your contents, either Home or Home Plus

Instead of an Index, you get a Table of Contents. The best guide to key features and benefits are scheduled on pages 4 and 5 of the NRMA booklet.

After two hours of reading, you are most likely to be completely exhausted and unable to define what type of insurance mix or stand-alone policy you want and what exactly any definable or specific benefits that policy contains.

Maybe this booklet should be taken apart and rewritten in clear language, where the different Building and Contents policies could be explained separately. To prevent confusion and to be clear about the details, other insurance providers use specific wording that outlines the period and percentage associated with the BSI Value for the *other benefits* they call *additional benefits*.

NRMA gives extra benefits and covers, if applicable, on top of the BSI Value, and that's included in the premium price.

> *Temporary accommodation for homeowners (Building's insurance policy) specified below under differences of sub-type—for 12-24 months.*
>
> *Temporary accommodation for tenants (or for strata scheme owners) Contents insurance policy—unspecified amount or period.*

I'm a strata scheme owner, and my NRMA Contents insurance policy doesn't list any amount for temporary accommodation.

> *Loss of rent for property owners/landlords (Building's insurance policy)—if a listed event causes loss or damage to your home and your tenants need to move out so it can be repaired or rebuilt. The rent you lose during the reasonable period it should take to repair or rebuild your home, for up to 12 months from when the event took place. Not covered if you or your family live in the home.*

The rent you lose should be in terms of the rental contract within the term of currency of the insurance policy.

> *Mortgage discharge costs (under Building's insurance policy)—if we agree to pay the building sum insured and you need to discharge any mortgage over your home. We pay the **administrative costs** to discharge any mortgage over your home.*

You don't have a choice. It will be carried out whether you want that to occur! The words "*you need*" are irrelevant.

Temporary accommodation for homeowners, Buildings insurance only—Home and Home Plus

If a listed event causes loss or damage to your home and you cannot live in your home and need to move out so it can be repaired or rebuilt.

Covered under Buildings insurance

Costs for temporary accommodation that we agree are reasonable and appropriate for you, your family, and your pets that you normally keep at your site.

That is related to a period of either 12 or 24 months—Home or Home plus—but not a percentage value of the BSI Value.

Any additional living expenses we agree are appropriate.

Costs to remove and store your contents and then return them to your home.

We pay these costs for the reasonable time we agree it should take to repair or rebuild your home.

We pay this benefit on top of your Building sum insured value.

Possibly not.

They don't say what the most you can get for the place you're staying at is, how much it's related to the BSI Value, and how long you can stay—12 or 24 months, depending on if you get the Home or Home Plus policy. It's up to the insurer to decide what's best for you and your family. It's hard to understand what the insurer is saying.

The Safety Net Home Plus type only

Payable on Buildings **and** Contents insurance policies. Why on Contents?

> *We pay more than your Buildings or General Contents sum insured if a listed event causes loss or damage to your home or contents and the cost to rebuild, repair or replace them is higher than your sum insured.*

What is the worth of this? Inflation won't make contents more valuable. If a *total loss* is considered, *other benefits*, like safety net value, are not paid out for buildings and contents.

Covered under Buildings insurance

> *Up to 25% of your Buildings sum insured to cover reasonable extra costs to repair or rebuild your home.*

It is not the responsibility of the insurer to rebuild your property. It needs to pay out the BSI Value, and you decide whether to rebuild.

> *For example, a widespread disaster leads to a high demand for building services, which increases your rebuilding costs. If your Buildings sum insured is $300,000, then we provide up to $75,000 on top of your Buildings sum insured to cover those extra costs.*

> *We pay this benefit on top of your Buildings sum insured.*

Add: If we consider a *total loss*, we pay zero *other benefits* such as safety net value. The meaning of *widespread disaster* is related to the meaning of the ICA Catastrophe Code wording, and this is not transparent.

Covered under Contents insurance

> *Up to 25% of your General Contents sum insured to cover reasonable extra costs to repair or replace your General Contents.*
>
> *We pay this benefit on top of your General Contents sum insured.*

Why? What determines this extra amount, if any? Under *total loss determination*, potentially no extra percentage value is payable—it's not specifically stated as it is for the BSI Value. This is not practical, realistic, or transparent.

Are these costs because of the *widespread nature of a listed event,* or just any event, not widespread? *Repair* suggests that the costs for repair could be paid out of the sum insured and no extra compensation is necessary. So, the above wording is again a misnomer! The wording is not practical, realistic, or transparent.

For example, it says:

> *A widespread disaster leads to a high demand for building services, which increases your rebuilding costs. If your Buildings sum insured is $300,000, then we provide up to $75,000 on top of your Buildings sum insured to cover those extra costs. We pay this benefit on top of your Buildings sum insured.*

That is not guaranteed! Refer to the extract from and commentary on the ICA Resilience Report, which I referenced above.

> *When a **total loss** is declared/considered by the insurer, and insurers have no option but to offer a **cash payment** rather than reinstate what has been damaged or destroyed because of the level of insurance the policyholder has taken out will not cover the cost of a repair or rebuild.*

There is no logical explanation of what *no option* implies. There is no basis for such an option. This is not transparent. *Damaged* and *destroyed* are different.

That *cash payment* will not include any additional benefits or safety net being added to the base BSI Value of the contract value, because the law affecting insurance does not make it so.

Covered under Contents Insurance

> *Up to 25% of your General Contents sum insured to cover reasonable extra costs to repair or replace your General Contents. We pay this benefit on top of your General Contents sum insured.*

This idea that general contents are in short supply is wrong—there are lots of shops that sell it, and it's unrelated to a jump in building prices because of a big event (declared disaster or otherwise) where prices for labor and materials go up because of scarcity and/or demand. Further, **contents** do not gain an inflation cost factor, and their value for damage or loss is the insured value stated in the certificate of insurance.

Costs for temporary accommodation

> *For tenants or strata scheme owners, we agree are reasonable and appropriate for you, your family, and your pets that you normally keep at your site.*

The maximum cost period varies between 12 months and 24 months, depending on the Home or Home Plus policy. No percentage value of the BSI Value is stated or limited. I have a NRMA contents insurance policy, and I was not asked whether I was a tenant or strata scheme owner, and my policy does not mention any value for temporary accommodation. My policy is therefore not transparent.

> *Any additional living expenses we agree are appropriate.*

What additional living expenses would be appropriate? How is the consumer to gauge what costs for temporary accommodation will be available from the policy, like a Stratum Residential Insurance policy—15% of the BSI Value—when this Contents policy does not provide any stated calculation percentage method?

Note: Policies have a validity period of 12 months, so is it possible for costs of living expenses to extend past the policy expiration date?

From the NRMA policy, example claim 3: Your home and contents are *destroyed*.

Note: There is no safety net payment involved here.

> *Your home and contents are insured for their full replacement value, are destroyed by fire. We agree to arrange temporary accommodation for the 6 months it will take to rebuild your home.*

Is that period practical or achievable **for a destruction scenario**?

As reported in *The Daily Telegraph* Friday January 5, 2024, the wait to build or renovate a home in Sydney has blown out to between 156 - 283 days for local council approval. That's an average of 219 days, which is over 6 months just for the approval process!

So now the cost for temporary accommodation is not either 12 or 24 months but 6 months. Worse, there is no safety net payout, meaning the loss of potentially 25% of the BSI Value to account for price increases because of an Event that is or could be widespread. And this example does not state what type of policy the calculation is for, either Home or Home Plus policy—merely building and contents insured for their full replacement value.

The rebuild price is not stated along with the BSI Value. There is no definition of what full replacement value is or any referenced formulation method!

Once again, using calculators to inform the replacement value is not advised.

The above example is not transparent.

Covered under Buildings insurance (Commentary on Home Plus Type)

> Up to 25% of your buildings sum insured to cover reasonable extra costs to **repair** or rebuild your home. For example, a **widespread disaster.**

A repair suggests that the BSI Value would be sufficient for that purpose and would not require an extra cash injection. *Widespread disaster* is now the ICA Catastrophe Code 2020 with the declaration of a catastrophe that could lead to a high demand for building services, which increases your rebuilding costs.

> If your Buildings sum insured is $300,000, then we provide **up to** $75,000 on top of your Buildings sum insured to cover those extra costs.

This may be because of an ICA Board Catastrophe Declaration under its industry catastrophe communications coordination strategy. That is not transparent.

> We pay this benefit on top of your Buildings sum insured.

Example 3: Your home and contents are destroyed—continued.

Policy type: Buildings and Contents insurance

Your home and contents are insured for their **full replacement value**, [and] are **destroyed** by fire. We agree to arrange temporary accommodation for the 6 months it will take to rebuild your home.

Building sum insured: $300,000.

Content's sum insured + $90,000.

Less basic excess - $1,000

Basic excess of $1000 Buildings and $500 contents

How we settle your claim

We choose to pay you directly for the loss. We pay you $399,400 made up as:

Buildings sum insured $300,000.

Contents sum insured +$90,000.

Less basic excess -$1000 (if you have combined your Buildings and Contents Insurance, then you only pay for one excess, whichever is the higher)

Subtotal $389,000

Plus, costs for temporary accommodation + $10,400 (we pay this on top of the building's sum insured)

Total $399,400.

There is no definition provided for *full replacement value*. The rebuild price has not been provided and is not stated. It is unreasonable for a home to be rebuilt within 6 months from the time of the event in case of, *for example, a* **widespread disaster.**

The insurer is not a clairvoyant and cannot predict that timeframe or the actual price of the rebuild.

What the insured should think is this:

- Deal with the contents first. You can take the payment of full value for contents to be a given. That part has been dispatched.
- The practical rebuild period for your home is 104 weeks. You will need temporary accommodation for at least that period. If you allow 15% of the BSI Value for that purpose, the rental value will amount to $45,000. To be more certain, you can find out the current weekly rental asking price from your local real estate agent for a comparable property in your local area to that which you have.
- You would have received $300,000 from the insurer for the payout for your home.
- Once your house plans have been approved by the authorities, and your funding is in order and approved, matching the rebuild price you get from your selected builder, you can start the construction process.

All that cannot happen in just 6 months. The insurer's proposition for temporary accommodation value is just 3.47% of the BSI Value and is not practical and not part of the contract terms. It is, therefore, not true.

So where are the timeframes, actual costs, practicality, fairness, honesty, and transparency in the above example? The only sensible part is the payout values you are insured for.

Example claim 4: Your home is destroyed—Home Plus policy.

> *Your home is **destroyed** by a bushfire. Your Buildings sum insured is $200,000 and the cost to rebuild is $250,000. We agree to arrange temporary accommodation for the 14 months it will take to rebuild your home.*

*We will increase the amount we pay you by **up to** 25% of your building sum insured under the 'Safety net' **other benefit** in your Home Plus policy.*

So, it looks like there's a difference between the insurance terms of *loss and total loss* and *destruction*, and it takes a lot of foresight to figure out the time needed to rebuild and the goodwill that comes with the safety net.

The insurer does not rebuild your home. It pays for damage repairs to reinstate the damaged part. The rebuilding part is your prerogative.

I think the insurer would have classified it as a total loss and paid out the BSI Value.

Policy type Buildings insurance—Home Plus policy

Building sum insured $200,000

Basic excess -$1,000

How we settle your claim

*We choose to pay you directly for the **destruction** of your home. We pay you $249,000:*

(Building sum insured $200,000 Plus (full) 25% safety net + $50,000 Less basic excess - minus $1,000.)

Subtotal $249,000 Plus costs for temporary accommodation + $20,000 (we pay this on top of the buildings sum insured)

Total $269,000.

That would equate to a 25.65% additional payout besides your BSI Value!

Here, temporary housing would be 10% of the BSI Value. Look at Example 3. The rent is 3.47% of the BSI Value.

Based on $750/wk. in 2022 for a 3-bedroom home in a Sydney rental zone for a similar property, the total for accommodation for 60 weeks (14 months) would amount to $45,000 less $20,000 provided by

NRMA, meaning a **shortfall of $25,000** as a minimum potential gap cost.

Whether it takes 6 months or 14 months, as seen from the various examples stated in the Booklet/PDS—refer to pages 85/86—the amounts set aside for accommodation are entirely at the insurer's discretion.

There is no logical explanation for the amounts of payouts for accommodation. This isn't clear for the insured, as the amounts should be kept the same as for Strata Residential Building Insurance. Typically, it's 15% of the BSI Value, though strata insurers like to emphasize that it's up to 15%. They won't pay expenses until they've been spent, and then only up to the Schedule value—if it's valid within the policy period or whatever other time frame or percentage value is specified, whichever is the lesser value.

> *We may pay you directly when you decide not to repair or rebuild your home,*
>
> *or you don't start repairing or rebuilding your home within 6 months from when the loss or damage takes place, or within any longer period we agreed to in writing.*
>
> *Maintaining and occupying your home: We will not cover loss, damage, injury, or death arising from:*
>
> *You are leaving your home unoccupied for 60 consecutive days or more and not maintaining it in a lived-in state by:*
>
>> *- Keeping the lawns mowed and garden tidy; stopping regular mail and newspaper deliveries; and organizing someone to check inside and outside your home at least once a week.*
>>
>> *- You are not maintaining your home in good repair and condition—this means that your home must be watertight, structurally sound, secure, and well maintained, and more.*

The above conditions and situations are for a repair or rebuild! This is nonsense, even if it is destroyed!

You must give evidence of loss and ownership. (Note: ICA Code of Practice 2020 overrides that requirement.)

When you take out a policy, or seek a quote, you *must* provide proof of identity—i.e., your driver's license with photo and residential address.

NRMA says: *We won't cover unreasonable delays to repair or rebuild your home.*

Don't forget, NRMA has control of everything, and the Insured can only do what's been agreed to. This outdated language and these methods belong in the past and should be changed by the NRMA.

Does this meet the ICA Code of Conduct's expectation that insurers be honest with the consumer? I don't think so. Does the new ICA Code of Practice 2020 sort this out? I don't think so.

Rebuilding Fees under Building Insurance Policy

> *The reasonable fees for architects, engineers, or surveyors and if a statutory authority served a notice on you before the* **listed event** *took place, are paid. The Insurer must pay the rebuilding fees before you make any arrangements.*

Presumably, the insurer will pay the fees as a percentage fee and other charges calculated on the **total cost of the project**. Maybe not. The fees will only be known after they have been spent on the completion of the works. Only the NRMA knows that one—a bit more clairvoyance involved. Who makes the arrangements? The NRMA is in charge. How will the *rebuilding fees* be paid before any arrangements are made? More clairvoyance.

Architect Fees and Charges are not accounted for in any of the examples (Example 3 or Example 4) of How We Settle Your Claim, shown above. Once again, I state it is not the responsibility of the insurer to rebuild your property. The cost of Architect Fees and Charges should have been costed into the BSI Value.

Commentary Conclusions

There are simply too many unknowns, conditions, limitations, and a lack of transparencies in this policy, which makes it a junk policy. The booklet/PDS is way too complicated. It's got a bunch of stuff jumbled together, some of it connected and some not, and it's not clear what the value of the extra benefits will be for building costs and temporary accommodation.

Everything is at the discretion of the NRMA *if you agree*.

It would benefit both the NRMA and the insured if this policy could be harmonized somewhat, like that of the Strata Residential Insurance Policy provisions.

I merely stress that this policy could be made simpler and clearer.

I've been a Contents policyholder for a while, and the NRMA has always been great at solving my Contents problems.

5.3 Commonwealth Bank Insurance Brochures and Forms[14]

Home Insurance Product Disclosure Statement (PDS) 1 October 2022 issued by Hollard Insurance.

> *This PDS and policy is provided by* **Hollard Insurance Partners Limited** *ABN 96 067 524 216, AFSL 235030 (Hollard).*
>
> *Established in* **South Africa** *in the 1980s to underwrite self-insurance programs for large corporate clients and banks, Hollard now comprises insurance businesses throughout Africa and Europe, India, China, Australia, and New Zealand.*
>
> *The Commonwealth Bank of Australia (CBA) is a distributor of Hollard's insurance products. CBA does not guarantee the obligations or performance of Hollard, or the products Hollard offers.*

Financial Claims Scheme and General Insurance Code of Practice Financial Claims Scheme states:

> *This product is a protected product under the Financial Claims Scheme (FCS). The FCS protects certain individuals in the event of an insurer becoming insolvent. In the unlikely event of Hollard Insurance Partners Limited becoming insolvent, you may access the FCS, provided you satisfy the eligibility criteria.*

---

14 https://www.commbank.com.au/insurance/brochures-forms.html#home
Product Disclosure Statements.
This Home Insurance Product Disclosure Statement applies to policies purchased and/or renewing on or after 01/10/2022
This CommInsure Home Insurance Product Disclosure Statement applies to policies purchased on the 10/04/2022 and renewing on/after the 22/05/2022
https://www.commbank.com.au/content/dam/commbank/personal/apply-on l i n e / download-printed-forms/home-insurance-pds.pdf

Hollard is a signatory to the Code. There is no mention of the ICA's catastrophe code in this document. To read the General Insurance Code of Practice or get additional information, visit codeofpractice.com.au.

CommInsure Excess and Discount Guide is shown for policies renewing after 22 May 2022. [15] This document provides information on several taxes that are applied in the various States and Territories in Australia. There are no taxes, levies or duties applied to CommInsure Home Insurance premiums for Norfolk Island policies.

All examples or illustrations in this PDS should show how certain benefits apply. This includes those shown in the Excess and Discount Guide[16]—an important document.

The values in the Excess and Discount Guide are variable because of the wording for *destruction, total loss, and constructive total loss*, where applicable, and may, therefore, change the outcome of the payable value.

They figure out all the benefits under the policy terms. The words and phrases in this PDS have special definitions, listed on pages 3 and 4. All figures in this PDS are in Australian dollars and include GST.

Check out the Insurer's Premium, Excess and Discount Guide to learn more about premiums, excesses, discounts, and how claims are settled. I recommend you do that as essential reading.

How this policy works

> *Home Insurance provides cover for the domestic home **you** or your **tenants** live in. This policy provides cover for a **defined list** of insurable events.*

---

15 https://docplayer.net/12707220-Comminsure-home-insurance-premium-excess-and-discount-guide.html

16 https://www.commbank.com.au/content/dam/commbank/personal/apply-online/download-printed-forms/comminsure-home-insurance-discount-guide.pdf

Home insurance provides cover for:
- *Insured Events. (See pages 29 to 38.)*
- *Additional Benefits. (See pages 39 to 46.)*

Additional Benefits.

Some Additional Benefits are paid within your sum insured, and some are paid besides. Limits on what we will pay also apply. For details on each, please read the relevant section.

Alternative accommodation costs.

This Additional Benefit applies to:
- *Residential Home Package—Building Cover.*
- *Residential Home Package—Contents Cover. [Note this needs to be a stratum titled property]*

What is covered [Note this is for reasonable accommodation costs.]

If we pay your claim because of an Insured Event and the damage at your insured address is so extensive that you can no longer live there, we will pay your reasonable accommodation costs:

- *if you own your insured address and have Building Cover; or*
- *if you own the insured address, and it is a stratum titled property, and your contents are insured by this policy.*

> *If we pay these costs, we will do so from the time your insured address becomes unlivable until it is livable again, **for up to a maximum of 52 weeks.***

Note: It does not state up to a maximum value, but only the period is mentioned from the time of the Event.

> *If you are renting the insured address as a tenant, and we pay your claim because of an Insured Event, we will pay the difference in rent incurred where you rent the insured address, and higher rent is charged for equivalent rental accommodation for you in the same area for the time remaining on your original lease.*
>
> *This Additional Benefit is payable on top of your nominated sum/s insured.*

Keep in mind, the place you move to may not be in the same area, since there may not be any vacancies in the same area, so that rent money you get may be less than what you must pay for accommodation that is not in the same area, resulting in gap costs.

Loss of rent costs

> *This Additional Benefit applies to:*
> - *Investment Home Package—Building Cover.*
> - *Investment Home Package—Contents Cover (Strata Titled properties only).*

Note: The Additional Benefit does not apply to Residential Home Package—Building Cover, or to Residential Home Package—Contents Cover.

For additional Optional Covers when selected by you. (See pages 47 to 52 of the policy Booklet).

However, cover is limited by **General Exclusions.** See pages 53 to 55 that apply to the whole policy. Forty-eight things are excluded. Please read all of them.

- *Limits on the amount we will cover for certain items and benefits. We offer the following options:*
- *Residential Home Package*
- *Investment Home Package*
- *Portable Contents Cover is available as a standalone policy or as an Optional Cover on a Residential Home Package. It is not available in an Investment Home Package.*

If you purchase our home insurance, we will send you a Certificate of Insurance which will include details of the Cover/s and Optional Cover/s you have selected and the Period of Insurance. It is important to read this entire PDS carefully to make sure you have the cover that suits your needs.

Summary of cover: Refer to pg. 5 for Insured Events and Additional Benefits.

Note: **Loss of Rent** is not covered by the Home Building Insurance product but by an Investment Home Package.

What is not covered

There is no cover under this Additional Benefit if you own the insured address, but it is not strata titled, and you haven't selected [Investment Home Package] --Building Cover. There is also no cover under this Additional Benefit where a General Exclusion applies (pages 53 to 55).

Gap Cover—Up to an additional 25% of your building sum insured (see pages 18 and 61).

> *Pg. 18—If your sum insured does not cover your loss, we will pay up to an additional 25% of the sum insured stated on your Certificate of Insurance towards the cost of repairing, rebuilding, or replacing your building and/or contents.* **This is called Gap Cover.**

It must be noted that this statement lacks transparency. Gap Cover does not apply with a total loss payout declaration by the Insurer. "Repairing" would suggest that you do not need Gap Cover.

Legal liability

> *Insured Event Maximum Claim Limit arising out of the same accident or underlying cause—See pages 37 to 38 Up to $20 million.*
>
> *Reasonable legal costs and expenses of lawyers we appoint acting on your behalf—See pages 37 to 38, up to $500,000.*

When to take out your policy

> *If you are buying a house, you may need to take out a policy before the purchase is completed. States and Territories have different laws about when the purchaser takes responsibility for the property. In some areas, it is from when the contracts are exchanged. In others, it is when the purchase is complete or when the purchaser takes possession. Check the requirements in your state or territory.*

Tell us about the changes at your address

> *During the Period of Insurance, you must tell us if anything on your Certificate of Insurance changes. This includes:*

- *proposed construction work at your insured address, including renovations, alterations, extensions, and structural improvements with a total retail value of more than $25,000 (whether this is the actual cost to you).*
- *if business, commercial or income-producing activities are going to be conducted at your insured address.*
- *if you have purchased a Residential Home Package and:*

    — are going to lease all or part of your insured address to someone else;

    — your insured address is going to be unoccupied for 60 consecutive days or more; or

If you tell us before you make any changes, we can tell you if we can continue to insure you:

- *under the same terms; or*
- *reduce the amount we pay in the event of a claim to the extent we have been prejudiced by your failure to tell us, potentially to zero; or*
- *cancel your policy.*

Important information about your sum/s insured

You can use the calculator on our website to estimate your insured sum.

I'd really advise against using this type of valuation. Get an insured value from a Registered Quantity Surveyor for the insurance replacement value of your building, but it's even better if you top up that base Replacement Value to cover for the catastrophe value—for destruction, catastrophe, total loss, and constructive total loss, to cover for extra costs after the Event which should also include for temporary accommodation for at least 104 weeks after your policy expiration date.

> *Your building and/or contents sum/s insured will be automatically adjusted on renewal to help keep pace with rising costs unless you tell us you do not want this to happen.*
>
> *Your Portable Contents sum/s insured are not adjusted by us. In all cases, you remain responsible for ensuring that the sum/s insured stated on your Certificate of Insurance is accurate. [Note: This is because contents do not gain any inflationary value.]*
>
> *This may cause you to need to increase or decrease your sum/s insured as you think is appropriate.* ***If you are underinsured, you may expose yourself to serious financial loss.***

Your building sum insured

> *Nominate a sum insured equal to the current total cost to rebuild it, inclusive of GST and all improvements (for example garages, driveways, and verandas) including an allowance for demolition and debris removal costs. You should also include an amount for all associated rebuilding costs, such as architectural, engineering, surveying, construction fees and legal expenses.*

That would cover for the base Replacement Value only and no other extra costs, such as escalation in building costs and temporary accommodation expense. This is where the 30% on top of the base replacement value comes in and protects you.

Your contents sum insured

> *Nominate a sum insured equal to the current total cost of replacing all your contents inclusive of GST. If you have selected both Portable Contents Cover and Contents Cover*

under a Residential Home Package, you do not need to include the value of your portable contents items in your contents sum insured.

How we settle a claim. Building, Contents and Portable Contents claims

If we pay your claim, we will, in consultation with you:

- *repair your damaged property where it is practicable and economical to do so.*
- *replace your lost or damaged property where it is not practicable and/or economical to repair it; or*
- *pay you the value that fairly represents your loss, as cash or a pre-paid store card*, up to the relevant sum insured stated on your current Certificate of Insurance applicable excess and/or outstanding premium, less the higher of your building or contents excesses.*

The portable contents cover excess will be payable if your claim also includes items insured.

If discount arrangements we have in place with suppliers result in us replacing or repairing any part of your building, contents, or portable contents for less than the sum insured or its retail value, we will not refund any premium or pay the difference.

This is just when you're replacing or repairing something in your building, possessions, or things you can take with you.

If we pay you in cash or store credit vouchers, we will not use any discount arrangements that may be available to us to reduce the amount we pay you.

Where your building and/or contents items are under finance and a total loss

In the event of a total loss, any payment made will first be made directly to the finance company/credit provider noted on your Certificate of Insurance, but only that part of the payment that relates to the property that is the subject of the finance/credit. The payment will be based on the amount they advise is outstanding. We will pay up to the sum insured less any applicable excess/es. Any remaining balance of your total loss claim that is left is then payable to you. After your claim is paid, if there's still money owed to the credit provider more than what you're insured for (minus any excesses), you've got to take care of the rest.

This is enabled due to the operation of the Third-Party Beneficiary Clause under the Insurance Contract Act 1984 (Commonwealth) Sec.48.

You will need to get legal advice on what countries this Commonwealth legislation applies to.

How we settle a claim (see page 60)

Gap Cover

*If we pay your claim and the costs for repairing, replacing, or rebuilding your building and/or contents exceed the sum/s insured stated on your Certificate of Insurance, we will pay these **actual costs** up to a further 25% of your sum/s insured. This is called Gap Cover.*

Gap Cover does not occur with a total loss payout.

Check out Example 3 in the CommInsure Excess and Discount Guide for policies renewing after 22 May 2022 for a simple explanation of this. This Guide contains examples of how the Insurer would settle your claim and should be viewed by all.

You should consider Example 3 shown in that Guide, as it shows what happens if you have a mortgage on your property—whether you want that to happen.

The application of a Third-Party Beneficiary Law applies in relation to the Insurance Contract Act 1984 (Commonwealth) Sec. 48, which could strip you of your insurance value.

This Act is super bad news for the person with the insurance policy and could mean the whole policy value is paid out to someone else.

Examples of how we may settle a claim

For examples of how we may settle a claim, please refer to the Premium, Excess and Discount Guide, which can be found at commbank.com.au/insurance home.[17]

What happens to your policy after a total loss?

Building and Contents claims

> *Where we decide that either your building and/or contents are a total loss, then the relevant cover (including any Optional Covers selected with this cover)* **will end on the day we pay the total sum insured** *with no refund for that component of the premium.*
>
> *If we settle a claim in any other way, the cover provided by this policy will continue to operate as stated in your Certificate of Insurance.*

That means:

> *If we pay these costs for reasonable accommodation, we will do so from the time your insured address becomes unlivable until it is livable again,* **for up to a maximum of 52 weeks.**

---

17   https://www.commbank.com.au/insurance.html

That is not transparent.

5.4 A Look at Youi Home Insurance Policy/PDS—called the "Home Product Disclosure Statement"[18]

Effective 4 September 2021. Youi Pty. Ltd. is an "Authorized policy" by APRA.

> *Youi Pty Ltd is an Australian registered company and is a wholly owned subsidiary of **Youi Holdings Pty Ltd**, a subsidiary of OUTsurance International Holdings Pty Limited.*
>
> *The ultimate holding company is OUTsurance Group Limited, which is part of the Rand Merchant Insurance Holdings Group (RMIH). It underwrites its policies, and its products include car, motorcycle, caravan, trailer, building and contents, watercraft, and business liability insurance. Youi exited the New Zealand market in 2019 and is now focused on growing its Australian market.*

The Youi Home Policy is clear. It says how much you'll need to pay and how much you won't, depending on the event. It also details extra stuff you can add to your policy and any extra options that you want that show up on your policy.

They state that the ICA Code of Practice, even though they agree to it, it isn't part of the contract. Right.

This policy doesn't mention anything about catastrophes, and there's no Gap Cover to fill in up to 25% of the BSI Value if the BSI isn't enough for rebuilding or replacing, like what you'd find in other policies. The other policies also say that if a total loss is declared, there won't be any Gap Cover or accommodation paid for 52 weeks.

---

[18]   https://www.youi.com.au/GetPDS?riskType=BUI

Sum Insured and Replacement Value

Your buildings and contents are covered on a new for old basis.

You select the sums insured. The contents sum is made of several components which are shown on your policy schedule.

To cover your buildings and contents

*You select an overall **current replacement value** for contents and for buildings.*

Buildings

*Allow for **the total cost of re-building**, including replacement of all fixtures, fittings, and structural improvements at the premises. The value of the land should be excluded because it is not covered.*

Unless you've budgeted for the building's full costs replacement value, the BSI Value won't include extra costs. This results in underinsurance!

These additional required costs and expense items to be covered to obviate underinsurance are included below.

Unless the market values of items mentioned below as **Extra Cover Items** are added to the BSI Value, amounts paid will be based on the lower BSI Value and probably will not support and sustain the costs and expenses that you would expect.

Extra Cover Items (for which you will pay extra)

Legal liability, temporary accommodation, insured events, burnout of electric motors, broken glass and ceramics, locks and keys, landlord's loss of rent, landlord's furnishings. Clean up and professional fees, contents outside, contents in transit, food spoilage, counselling services.

Note: Extra cover and values and exclusions for all those **extra cost items** are explained. Refer to the PDS.

The 100% estimated catastrophe full costs BSI Value that I have shown includes Architect Fees and Charges, Debris removal costs, escalated building costs and loss of rent/temporary accommodation.

General exclusions

These general exclusions apply to all sections of your policy. Refer to page 28 of the policy, which has 48 exclusions listed.

How we settle your claim

*The most we will pay is the sum insured noted on your policy schedule, or any applicable policy limits as noted in this PDS, plus any applicable amounts under the **Extra Cover** section, and any additional amounts under any **Optional Covers** which have been added to your policy.*

Claiming

About your cover Important Information, go to contents page 32.

The settlement options below only apply where you hold cover for the relevant insured property under your policy.

1. **If you are claiming for buildings**

    If we can, we will settle your buildings claim by:
    - *repairing the damaged parts of your buildings if it is both possible for the parts to be repaired and economical for us to repair those parts because the cost of repair is less than the cost of rebuilding; or*
    - *rebuilding the damaged part of your buildings if it is not possible for those parts to be repaired or not economical for us to repair those parts because the cost of repair is more than the cost of rebuilding.*

    If we cannot repair or rebuild the damaged part of your buildings, we will pay you an amount equal to the reasonable cost that you would incur to repair or rebuild [the damaged part of] the buildings up to the limits noted in your policy. We will undertake a search of the market to determine what this cost would be in your area, based on factors including work and comparison quotes from repairers or builders. We can use a combination of the above settlement methods if we can repair or rebuild the damaged part of your buildings.

That is a vast grey area and appears to me to be a waste of everyone's time. What should happen is that the BSI Value should be paid out in full, immediately. The Architect Fees and Charges for fictitious work and builder's quotes should be removed because it wastes everyone's time and results in unconscionable conduct.

2. **If you are claiming for contents**

    We will settle your contents claim if we can.
    - *if the item has been lost, replace the lost item. [with a similar matching item]*

> - *if the item has been damaged, repairing the damaged item if it is both possible for it to be repaired and economical for us to repair it because the cost of repair [of the damaged item] is less than the cost of replacement.*
>
> *If we cannot repair or replace your contents, we will pay you an amount equal to the reasonable cost **you would incur** to repair or replace your contents up to the limits noted in your policy.*
>
> *We will undertake a search of the market to determine what this cost would be in your area, based on factors including comparison quotes from repairers or suppliers. We will make the payment to you via a store credit or voucher through our service providers, or cash where our service providers are not in your area. If we can repair or replace some of your damaged items, we can use a combination of the above settlement methods.*

Carrying out a fictitious search of the market would be time-consuming, practically impossible to describe/specify that repair/replacement item, and a waste of everyone's time. This is not a sensible settlement solution and is a nonsense.

The full amount, as noted in the schedule, should be paid out. Cut out the haggle and the clairvoyance part as to the cost **you would incur** to repair or replace your contents, as that is likely impossible to find out.

Before Claiming, go to contents page 33.

If we pay the sum insured.

> *If we pay you the building's sum insured because of an incident, then we will cancel your building's cover.*

> *We will cancel your contents cover if we pay you the sum insured.*
>
> *This is because we will have fulfilled our contract with you by making this payment.*

Finally, we have some logic!

3. Specified items.

> *If claiming for an item that has been individually specified in your policy, we will pay the replacement cost of the item **up to** the amount you have selected.*

Note: It may not be possible to match the specified article's replacement cost, the full insured value should be paid out—not anything less or "up to." The wording should be specific.

4. How repairs are done

> *If your claim is accepted and your buildings and contents can be repaired by us, we will arrange for these repairs to be undertaken by a member from our network of repairers.*
>
> *With buildings repairs, you may need to enter a separate domestic building contract with the repairer. Refer to the Sum Insured and Replacement Value section and Matching Materials section for further details on the materials we use when rebuilding, replacing, or repairing your buildings or contents.*

Note: Buildings and Contents require different resolutions with "repairing, replacement, or rebuilding."

5. Salvage

Any property that we pay for, repair, or replace becomes our legal property when we settle your claim. This includes any undamaged property that is part of a pair or set.

Note: The wording of this clause is irresponsible when referring to any property. This clause is atypical and seemingly not applicable in other similar insurance policies.

6. Free automatic reinstatement of cover

Where we settle your claim for any amount less than the full sum insured on your policy, we will automatically reinstate the sum insured, to the level it was prior to the claim occurring, for the rest of the contract period. You will not be charged an additional premium for this reinstatement.

7. Our right to recovery

*After we pay a claim under this policy, we can decide to begin or defend a legal action in your name to recover money from the **person or entity** that caused loss, damage, or liability. You must give us all the help we need to do this, such as answering questions we ask. If we recover money that belongs to you and is not part of the claim we paid, we will give this to you.*

8. Rights of a financier

For any payment we make to settle your claim, we may first pay in full any sum owed to a financier of your insured property from the settlement amount. If we do this, any remaining balance will be paid to you.

Extra cover for Legal Liability and Buildings is the most important thing to consider if it is included as extra cover, and my commentary is noted.

Extra cover

The extra covers listed below are automatically included in your policy unless it is stated to only apply to buildings or contents cover specifically. Where applicable, the most we will pay for each claim is noted.

1. **Legal Liability.**
2. **Buildings**

    Under your buildings policy, your legal liability arising from an accident that results in death, bodily injury, or damage to **property of a third party** *if:*

    - *the accident arises in connection with you owning the premises.*
    - *the accident occurred during the term of your buildings policy; and*
    - *the accident occurred at the premises. The most we will pay for each claim is $20,000,000.*

    Note: Including all legal and defense costs and GST.

3. **Contents**

    Under your contents policy, your legal liability arising from an accident that results in death, bodily injury, or damage to **property of a third party** *if:*

- *the accident does not arise in connection with you owning a building.*
- *the accident arises in relation to you.*

Note: Presumably to you or a third party. Refer to the exclusion paragraph below.

- *The accident occurred during the term of your contents policy; and*
- *the accident occurred anywhere in Australia. The most we will pay for each claim is $20,000,000.*

Note: Including all legal and defense costs and GST. This is dissimilar to Hollard, where $500,000 may also be paid for legal expenses.

2. Temporary Accommodation: Insured Events

The following is covered if it is included as extra cover.

Buildings

Where the premises is owner-occupied, the actual cost you incur for your suitable temporary accommodation for a period of up to 12 months, while your buildings are being repaired or rebuilt, if you cannot live at the premises after an insured event for which a claim is accepted under your buildings policy and we agree that temporary accommodation is required.

Note: If it is included and paid for as extra cover and if there is a "total loss" declared, you will get zero value for loss of rent or temporary accommodation.

The most we will pay for each claim is 12% of the building's sum insured, which includes up to:

- *4 weeks in suitable emergency or short-term accommodation.*
- *48 weeks in suitable residential accommodation at a similar standard to your home; and*
- *the reasonable and necessary costs for:*
  - *redirection of mail from the insured premises for up to 12 months.*
  - *utility connection costs at the temporary accommodation residence; and*
  - *relocation of your contents to and from the temporary accommodation residence if you have contents cover under this policy. We will also pay up to $250 per month for pet accommodation, up to a limit of $3,000, for each claim.*

Suitable accommodation

Will be assessed based on factors including number of household members, proximity to the insured property, parking requirements and availability.

Note: The wording "Suitable accommodation" does not mean comparable accommodation in a similar area. It means what the insurer thinks is suitable.

This policy is dissimilar to Hollard, as there are now up to 52 weeks **and** up to 12% of the BSI Value attached to this clause, meaning the lesser value applies.

Because of circumstances, temporary accommodation may only be available in surrounding areas where no reasonably priced accommodation is available in your immediate area.

Note: This clause might add to your stress and anxiety, because any additional expense greater than that provided will need to be funded by you. Further, if you do not **repair or rebuild** your property after an insured event for which a claim is accepted, you will **not get compensation** for temporary accommodation **or** loss of rent, where you have informed the insurer that you are a landlord.

> *The most we will pay in total for each claim is 12% of the building's sum insured plus up to $2,500 for pet accommodation.*

Kindly note that there is a provision that limits the payment of rent loss or temporary accommodation, notwithstanding its inclusion as an extra cover. Payment will be denied if you do not repair or rebuild. The most the insurer will pay for each claim is 12% of the building's sum insured.

This includes **up to**

- 4 weeks in a suitable emergency or short-term accommodation.
- 48 weeks in suitable residential accommodation at a similar standard to your home while you repair or rebuild after an event for which a claim is accepted.

If costs for accommodation exceed 12% of the BSI Value, **gap costs** will be inevitable, but the insured needs to budget for that expense for at least 104 weeks—the period it may take to rebuild—and include this value into the total BSI Value to be assured that funding from the policy will account for that purpose.

The way to budget for that expense is to calculate the value for temporary rental accommodation to last for at least 104 weeks. Thus, if the current rental value of your existing property, before the event, is $700/week, that total amount required from the insurance value will be 700 x 104 = $72,800.

$700/week rent value also assumes that the Market Sale Value of your existing home and land value is 700 x 52 = 36400 x 100 divided by 3 = $1,213,333.00.

This equation also works the other way round. Thus, $1,213,333.00 multiplied by 3 divided by 100, and divide that total by 52 = $699.99.

There is no correlation between market sale value and insurance replacement value, but there is a relationship between *rental value and the minimum insurance replacement value* you should have for a residential property.

This insurance policy does not state any insurance sum value example for the 12% additional benefit value, as **extra cover** you have paid for in the premium, to be evaluated for comparison.

Hypothetically, taking the market sale value as your assumed insured sum value, 12% of that value would amount to $1,213,333.00 x 12% = $145,600.

The budgeted assumed usual amount value, compared to **strata insurance**, for loss of rent/temporary accommodation value is **15% of the sum insured value**, and this would amount to, equivalently, $1,213,333.00 x 15% = $182,000.

That budgeted shortfall between 12% and 15% would amount to c. -$36,400, which would be the potential gap cost/expense you might need to fund from savings or increased mortgage value.

Therefore, the 12% you might get might **not support and sustain** the costs and expense of being unable to live at your home in the year 2023 in Sydney. In fact, the rental value for a comparable house, as mentioned above, is more like a median rental cost of $820 – >$1000 per week in the Sydney post code 2120—January to May 2023—depending on the type and quality of accommodation you choose to rent and is available.

To avoid **underinsurance**, calculate the loss of rent/temporary accommodation amount value, as mentioned above, and divide that total by 15%, not 12%, to arrive at the **BSI Value.** Thus, 700 x 104 weeks/15% = $485,333 to be the augmented replacement value. If your BSI Value is less than that figure, you are underinsured.

Adjust that value to match the prevailing annual rental inflation rate for the current and next year..

The moral of this tale is: Don't count on policy perks to cover your temporary housing costs. Confirm that the BSI Value you pick can cover those costs for 104 weeks by doing the math above and add the assumed rental fees for displacement value to increase the minimum replacement value. You might add 10% besides the above rental requirement to account for the inflation factor over 104 weeks. Adjust that percentage value to match the prevailing inflation or CPI Rate for the current and next year.

Contents with Strata title

> *With a stratum title building, when a body corporate takes out building insurance, we will pay the actual cost you incur for your suitable temporary accommodation* ***for a period of up to 52 weeks.***
>
> *The most we will pay for **1 month's accommodation** on each claim is 1% of the contents sum insured, plus up to $250 for pet accommodation. The most we will pay in total for each claim is 12% of the contents sum insured, plus up to $3,000 for pet accommodation.*

A "fix up" and a "redo" are two different things. The strata entity oversees the rebuild, and the contents policy insurer should pay out 12% of the CSI Value for rent/temporary accommodation costs. It'll probably take 104 weeks or more to finish the rebuilding.

A **rebuild process** with a stratum title building probably won't be finished in 52 weeks, since the Owners' Corporation oversees it.

For the **repair process**, the compensation *should be described* as the actual cost you incur for suitable temporary accommodation **for a period of up to 52 weeks or up to 12% of the CSI Value, whichever is the lesser value.**

You'll have to pay the gap cost if the time/percentage isn't enough. Again, it's important to boost the BSI Value by at least 15% to cover 104 weeks of accommodation. Do not rely on Contents insurance to pay for your alternate accommodation needs.

Tenants with Strata title

> *Where you are the **tenant at the premises**, we will pay for the additional rent costs incurred for **suitable** [and available] **temporary accommodation** for up to 1 month, and the most we will pay for **1 month's accommodation** on each claim is 1% of the contents sum insured, plus up to $250 for pet accommodation.*
>
> ***Suitable accommodation** will be assessed based on factors including number of household members, proximity to the insured property, parking requirements and availability.*

Note: The concerning part of this is that "if there is no intention to repair or rebuild the buildings," you will not get any value for the cost of temporary accommodation where you are a TENANT and **you do not** also have a CONTENTS policy with Youi. So, wherever you live, if you can't live in your tenanted/leased house, you will bear the full cost of that temporary accommodation, meaning you will effectively pay "double rent"—lease agreement cost for the residue period of the lease, and the new temporary accommodation expense.

The Owners' Corporation, not you, needs to decide whether they're going to repair or rebuild, so these restrictions aren't right.

What is not covered with Contents for the cost of temporary accommodation

With a strata title building, and a body corporate takes out building insurance and you have a contents policy with Youi.

Where the premises are a Strata Title building, and a body corporate takes out building insurance; the actual cost you incur for your reasonably priced temporary accommodation for a period of up to 52 weeks while your buildings are being repaired or rebuilt.

If you cannot live at the premises after an insured event for which a claim is accepted under your contents policy with Youi and we agree that temporary accommodation is required.

The most we will pay for 4 weeks accommodation on each claim is 1% of the contents sum insured plus up to $250 for pet accommodation.

Four weeks' accommodation at 1% of the CSI Value (contents sum insured), say $100,000, equates to c. $1000 for 4 weeks.

Median rent in the 2120 Sydney area is $820 – >$1000 a week, so you'd face a sizeable gap in the CSI Value.

The most we will pay in total for each claim is 12% of the contents sum insured plus up to $2,500 for pet accommodation.

Note: Similarly, on the hypothetical value $100,000 CSI Value, 12% is $12,000 for 52 weeks, thus the minimum hypothetical $820/wk. is $42,640 less $12,000 = c. -$30,640 gap cost to you personally.

If there is no repair or rebuild, and/or a **total loss** is declared by Youi, you get no value for loss of rent/temporary accommodation costs and expenses.

Temporary Accommodation: Emergency Evacuation What is covered

The actual cost you incur (but limited to 30 days and an excess of $400 is payable) for your reasonably priced temporary accommodation in relation to an emergency where the relevant local authority either instructed you to evacuate or prevented you from accessing the premises up to the day you may return to the premises if you have combined Buildings and Contents cover.

Landlord's Loss of Rent What is covered

Buildings

Where your building is rented out and no longer safe to live in, we will pay a reasonable rental amount for the period it cannot be rented out up to a maximum of 52 weeks.

We will pay the reasonable rental loss amount for the remaining rental contract period and if it cannot be rented out thereafter, the equivalent value of rent loss value will be for 52 weeks after the event.

Payment for Loss of Rent should follow the lease agreement value and period, not exceeding 52 weeks or the actual net rental income loss, with a maximum of 12% of the BSI Value plus $2,500 for pet accommodation.

Contents

The most we will pay if the building is a Strata Title and a body corporate takes out building insurance, the actual

> *current net rental income up to a maximum of $2,000 per month for each claim where loss or damage was caused by an insured event.*

About the Code:

> *The Code sets out the standards that general insurers must meet when providing services to their customers, such as being honest.*

As of 2023, the absence of transparency and the lack of ASIC approval regarding the inclusion of a voluntary Code of Practice policy in any insurance policy wording/PDS continues to be prevalent.

> *The Code review process is there to ensure that the Code remains relevant and continues to meet the needs of consumers.*

Evidently, the ICA carried out these evaluations for internal use only, devoid of any input from informed consumers.

> *The Code raises customer service standards in the general insurance industry, and to protect the rights of consumers.*

The obligation to ensure the protection of rights lies with the policy providers, not with the consumers. The standards are not identical to the objectives and principles concerning the customer. In case of relevance, standards would aim at ensuring that additional expenses are uniformly considered in the PDSs of insurance policies.

> *These standards apply when selling insurance, dealing with insurance claims, **responding to catastrophes** and disasters, and handling complaints.*

Irrespective of the established criteria, the specifics of each policy are consistently unique. Irrespective of the activation of the catastrophe clause within an insurance policy, the response to "catastrophe" adheres to the ICA Catastrophe Code policy, ICA Board Declaration policy, or any other third-party state of emergency declaration clause linked to the State.

Note: Information in this section summarizes the catastrophe provisions in the Code. It is recommended that anyone who has experienced a catastrophe reviews **the Catastrophes** section in the Code (Section 9) for full details. Upon accessing the website, the term catastrophe pertains solely to Retail Insurance.

Catastrophes:

> *The Code of Practice commits insurers to respond to catastrophes efficiently, professionally, and compassionately.*
>
> *The ICA will declare an event to be a catastrophe when it results in many claims and involves multiple insurers.*

It is not advisable to have an external policy condition in place for the insurance contract to determine the contract terms efficiently. According to the Commonwealth Law Insurance Contract Act of 1984, it is neither efficient nor correct to include any wording in the policy or circumstance that pertains to a third-party, as the contract is only between the insurer and the insured.

This clause not only cannot protect the rights of the insured party but also deprives them of any rights they may have had concerning the Building Valuation Schedule Offer and the specified insured sum values stated in the Schedule and/or Certificate, or the language within its PDS.

The conclusion is diabolical and is far removed from the meaning of a catastrophic situation, which involves destruction, total loss, and constructive total loss. The current unfortunate situation may persist due to the lack of approval of the Code by ASIC and the absence of any legislative framework defining terms such as destruction, catastrophe, total loss, or constructive total loss.

> *A catastrophe is most declared after an extreme weather event such as a severe cyclone, bushfire, flood, or storm.*

It should be noted that the events listed are not exhaustive of all defined events outlined in any insurance policy wording/PDS, and it is possible for loss, damage, or destruction, or constructive total loss to occur, regardless of whether a Catastrophe Code declaration or ICA Board Declaration has been made.

The exclusion of Home Building Insurance and Contents Insurance from the Insurance Council of Australia's jurisdiction is justifiable. This is due to the ICA's intervention in Third-Party Catastrophe Clause policies, which have resulted in a conflict of interest.

The determinations and terms established by the ICA, coupled with its policies, do not form a legal insurance policy/PDS condition provision, nor do they constitute a valid entity in any Home Building Insurance or Contents Insurance policy contract wording. This is not a legal interpretation, but a practical and commonsense one.

Longitude, a major Stratum residential insurance provider, employs a different catastrophe clause terminology—a state declaration of a state of emergency.

The Youi Home insurance policy states openly that it does not employ the ICA Code of Practice, although it is a signatory of the ICA Code of Practice.

To put it briefly, the ICA Catastrophe Code displays a considerable tendency and has the potential to have an adverse impact on the policyholders. It represents a significant conflict of interest within the insurance provider industry because the additional benefits outlined in the policy are directly affected by both the ICA Catastrophe Code and the ICA Board Declaration, and the cover-holder may also be implicated if they comply with Lloyd's directives and cannot protect against conflicts of interest.

My advocacy is for ASIC to mandate the ICA Code of Practice as a prerequisite for its approval and oversight. The aim is to eliminate the catastrophe clause definition or declaration by the ICA from being present in any policy wording, including any State-based catastrophe clause that pertains to a state of emergency and/or state-authorized evacuation announcement.

This is because the conditional meaning and application of a policy's catastrophe condition and related additional benefits and compensation costs have an adverse effect on the consumer.

The provisions also encompass the deduction of any financial benefits furnished by the State. It is not the policy of the State to provide subsidies to insurance providers.

Don't wait for ASIC to change this appalling situation. My suggestion to combat the denial of payment for the additional benefits is to obtain insurance coverage for *100% of the catastrophe estimated full costs BSI Value.*

Chapter Six

SUGGESTIONS FOR INNOVATION

 ## 6.1 GENERAL AND KEY POINTS

- Below, I have described a legislative, structural improvement for determining the correct BSI Value payout to full costs value, which should include the additional benefits or extra costs with *destruction, catastrophe, total loss, and constructive total loss.*

- If the law were changed, this would help body corporates and the general homeowner to get the rightful amount of insurance coverage, with the provision of the somewhat accurate 100% catastrophe estimated full costs BSI Value.

- The purpose of the subsequent commentary is to provide guidance to both consumers and legislators in differentiating the values for payout of several insured sums, which are funded in the BSI Value.

- Due to deficient and unsuitable legislation, the minimum replacement value disregards ancillary extra costs with destruction, catastrophe, total loss, or constructive total loss. My advocacy stems from the law's lack of protection for these values.

- In the absence of legal protection for these additional costs, an augmentation of a minimum of 30% to the Minimum Replacement Value is recommended to compensate for the missing funding for extra costs.

6.2 The Insurance Act 1973 (Commonwealth) Sec.12, Obtaining an Authorization, states:[19]

(4) If The Australian Prudential Regulatory Authority (APRA) allows an applicant, APRA must:

(a) give written notice to the applicant; and

(b) ensure that notice of the Authorization is published in the Gazette.

It is recommended that this be included in the "important information" section at the beginning of the Insurance Policy PDS.

Inclusion and dating of authorization within the policy wording/PDS is of utmost importance and must be carried out every time the policy wording/PDS undergoes modification.

Holding an AFS license does NOT provide a guarantee of the probity or quality of the licensee's services.

I would like to inquire about the measures implemented to ensure protection for the consumer/insured. What is the key function of a Regulatory Authority?

6.3 APRA Register of Approved General Insurance[20]

The following is a list of approved insurance providers, current as of May 2020, discussed in this work.

Alliance Australia Insurance Ltd.

AAI Ltd.

AIG Australia Ltd.

Chubb Insurance Australia Ltd.

QBE Insurance Australia Ltd.

---

19 http://classic.austlii.edu.au/au/legis/cth/consol_act/ia1973116/

20 https://www.apra.gov.au/register-of-general-insuranceinsurance

Youi Pty. Ltd.

Swiss Reinsurance Company Ltd.

Swiss Re International SE

Commonwealth Insurance Ltd -The Commonwealth Bank of Australia (CBA) is a distributor of Hollard's insurance products.

Please be informed that I encountered challenges locating the APRA-specific authorization of the insurance provider at the beginning of the policy/PDS.

Information regarding Lloyd's operations in Australia can be accessed by clicking on the APRA reference.

6.4 The Insurance Contracts Act 1984 Sec. 44 Should be Reviewed

I'm pushing for the Insurance Contracts Act 1984 (Commonwealth) Sec. 44 to be looked at again regarding Replacement Value for real estate value, since the proportional Average Provision Rule doesn't work for real estate insurance replacement value, and I can show why.

Suggested changes to this Act's Sec. 44 wording are described below.

Let's get rid of the Average Clause in the Insurance Policy PDS for real estate property to be honest and to stop any speculation and deception. The below narrative proves it.

Consumer protection *regarding* **insurance** *policies:*[21]

> *(1) An insurer may not rely on an **average provision** included in a contract of general insurance unless, **before** the contract was entered, the insurer clearly informed the insured in **writing** of the provision including whether the provision is based on indemnity or on*

---

21 http://www6.austlii.edu.au/cgi-bin/viewdoc/au/legis/cth/consol_act/ica1984220/s44.html

replacement ***value*** of the property that is the subject-matter of the contract;

(2) Where the **sum insured** regarding property that is the subject-matter of a contract of general insurance that provides insurance cover regarding loss of or damage to a building *[***intangible asset – bold emphasis added***]* used primarily and principally as a residence for the insured, for persons with whom the insured has a family or personal relationship, or for both the insured and such persons, or loss of or damage to the contents *[***tangible asset – bold emphasis added***]* of such a building, or both, is not less than 80% of the ***value***.

(3) Where: the **Sum Insured value** that is the subject-matter of such a contract **is less than** 80% of the ***value*** of the property and but for this ***subsection***, an average provision included in the contract would have the effect of reducing the liability of the insurer regarding loss of or damage to the property to an amount that is less than the amount found under the formula.

In (3) above, there is a difference between *Sum Insured Value* and *80% of the value of the property*. These differences are not described in the contract of insurance because the specialist insurance valuer practitioner's Building Insurance Valuation Report is not an essential part of the contract terms regarding values. This leads to the phenomenon that the BSI Value may not be the minimum replacement value but a higher value.

The PDS reference within the Longitude Strata Residential Insurance policy shows that the value is contingent upon the BSI Value being less than 80% of the replacement value immediately prior to the Event. If that is the scenario, then the percentage values for the additional benefits will become zero instead of being reduced from 80% to 65%

(which implies a reduction of 15% in the policy's additional benefits) when the additional benefits' value can be fully reduced to zero upon reaching a difference in value of 65%—which is the minimum replacement value just before the Event divided by the BSI Value that was chosen. Kindly refer to Table 4.1 where this is elaborated.

Replacement Value cannot be ascertained due to the absence of a legally sourced Building Insurance Valuation Report contract document to substantiate it. The specialist insurance valuer practitioner is also not defined by any laws, including the DBP Act 2020.

The Insurance Contract Act 1984 Sec.44 lays out that the value should be the one right before the event when the contract was signed. The NSW Strata Act calls this "at least the minimum replacement value," so:

"value", *in relation to property, means:*

(a) *if the relevant contract provides for indemnifying the insured regarding loss of or damage to the property, the indemnity **value** of the property;* [**tangible asset, goods and chattels—emphasis wording added**] *or*

(b) *if the relevant contract provides for reinstatement or replacement of the property, the reinstatement or replacement **value** of the property* [**intangible asset—building sum insured value - emphasis wording added**]; *when the relevant contract was entered."*

The Act wording in (b) above now states that for real estate, that value is the reinstatement or replacement value of the property when the contract was entered. *That value could be any value selected as the BSI Value,* but the NSW Strata Act and regulations state that value as being at least the minimum replacement value immediately prior to the Event.

Check out Table. 4.1 for the insurance value formula where the estimated sum immediately prior to the event—the PAA value—and the FAA Sum Insured Values, are stated.

The Commonwealth Insurance Contract Act Sec. 44 jumbles together both intangibles and tangibles in the Average Rule.

I think that Rule is wrong and doesn't work because it's not specific about the insurance values for real estate property when the contract was entered.

The insurance value, mentioned above, is at least the minimum replacement value of real estate at the time the contract was entered, as per the SSMR 2016 Reg. 39, insurance, or the actual insurance contract BSI Value selected by the insured, which may be a greater value.

Those two values could mean the minimum replacement value immediately prior to the Event, and the BSI Value which may be augmented to include the additional benefits or extra costs associated with building escalated costs and for loss of rent/temporary accommodation and possibly extended accommodation expense and other building code compliance costing.

Table.4.1 shows that the *higher* the BSI Value is in relation to the minimum replacement value, the *lower* the percentage difference below 80% will be when comparing the selected actual BSI Value—the FAA Value, to the minimum replacement value—the PAA Value.

The **Formula**, as described in the Insurance Contract Act 1984 Sec. 44, **is unworkable** for real estate building insurance replacement value, as the **higher the BSI Value** is in relation to the minimum replacement value, *at the time the relevant contract was entered,* the **lower** the percentage value below 80% will be—and increasingly so.

This effectively may negate the contract terms for catastrophe schedule sums insured value from being operative, which **may** include Sums Insured for *escalated building costs value* **and** for *loss of rent/temporary accommodation cost and expense value,* as per the policy PDS.

Check out the Building Insurance Valuation Report Table. The Strata Legislation (NSW) should require the Building Insurance Valuation Report Table to have the formulation of the minimum replacement BSI Value, as in Table. 4.1, formulated from the make-up of costs shown in the SSMR NSW 2016 Reg. 39—insurance, and the **100% of the estimated catastrophe full costs value** to form part of the documentation showing the contract values.

From the example in Valuation Table, Fig. 4.1, the figures are:

4220276 /5486359 = 76.92%, which fails the 80% rule. This shows how unworkable the 80% Average Provision Rule is and how it won't work for determining the real estate insurance values available under the catastrophe clauses.

If this Rule were to be applied, it would mean, with the above BSI Value reduction below 80%, that is 76.92%, that the insured would suffer a reduction of 3.08% for all the Additional Benefits stated in the Schedule because of that catastrophe clause application. This would happen because of being insured for the estimated FULL COSTS! How nuts would that be?

From the Formula: *"(Insurance Contracts Act 1984 (Commonwealth) Sec. 44:*

$$\frac{AS}{P}$$

[This formula means "A" multiplied by "S" divided by "P"]

*where **A** is the number of dollars equal to the amount of the loss or damage.*

One would not know what the loss or damage is initially. The phrase is not specific as to minimum insurance replacement value or BSI Value, the estimated catastrophe costs replacement value equivalent to the FAA or the actual real costs **determined after**

repair, rebuild, replacement, or replacement on another site, and all after these have been completed.

S is the amount of the sum insured under the contract regarding the property [the contract BSI Value].

P is 80% of the number of dollars equal to the value.

Value here means reinstatement or replacement value when the contract was entered and effectively means the minimum replacement value or PAA Value but could mean a greater value than the minimum replacement value immediately prior to the Event, when the contract was entered.

If the law is changed to include the Building Insurance Valuation Formulation Table/Report as a crucial part of the Building Insurance Valuation Schedule of Offer for the premises, the Valuation information would then provide values for both the minimum insurance value and the estimated full costs value, which could be the selected BSI Value. The insurer's liability for the additional benefits sum insured percentage values would then be in relation to the Sum Insured Value when the contract was entered.

The 80% Average Provision Rule would then be inoperable and irrelevant as the values of the contract are clearly stated, stopping fictional values and any speculation as to values of the contract.

The current insurance contract policy (Longitude) catastrophe clause is so worded that the insured would not get their full extra costs compensation rights because of the definition and limitations of the *catastrophe clause* and the *limitation of liability clause* in the NSW Legislative provisions that allows the insurer to do as it pleases. These clauses in the policy PDS and law are unfair and don't work for the insured.

6.5 Reference to the Commonwealth Insurance Contracts Act 1984 Sec. 48

This section gives meanings to:

> A *Third-party beneficiary*, under a contract of insurance, means a person who is not a party to the contract but is specified or referred to in the contract, whether by name or otherwise, as a person to whom the benefit of the insurance cover provided by the contract extends.

This is a total injustice to the insured, who took out the policy, because the policy value can be reduced to nothing without the insured's agreement.

6.6 The NSW Strata Act and Regulations for Insurance use an Inaccurate Valuation Approach.

> *If the building is destroyed, the building is to be rebuilt or replaced so that the condition of every part of the rebuilt or replacement building is not worse or less extensive than that part when new.*

Judging by my commentary above, you will note how way off this statement is.

The *replacement value valuation extent* of the building when it was "new" implies an Indemnity Value valuation method, diminishing the value to the time the building was built when new. The minimum replacement value may prove insufficient for the reconstruction or substitution of the building. *It is up to the insured party to decide whether to rebuild.*

The second clause—refer to NSW Strata Act Sec. 161 (2) wording below—regarding the **"limitation of liability"** of the insurer has the effect of reducing the BSI Value, whatever value it is to an indemnity value assessment of replacement cost with *either partial or full reinstatement/replacement or replacement on another site* situation.

In any cash settlement offer involving *total loss* declaration, extra costs are excluded if they are not built into the BSI Value.

The limitation of the liability clause has an **Adverse Effect** in this typology legislation.

Section 161 (2) wording is:

> *In terms of SSMA Act NSW 2015 Cl. 161 (2):* **'Limited sum liability'** *Instead of providing for* **work and payments** *being made if a* **building** *is destroyed or damaged, the* **damage policy** *may limit the liability of the insurer in that event to an amount specified in the policy. The amount must not be less than an amount calculated under the regulations.*

What it should account for is this: Provide for **work and payments** being *catastrophe schedule value* and *loss of rent/temporary accommodation schedule value* as stated and shown in the Building Insurance Valuation Schedule of Offer.

The Commonwealth Insurance Contract Act 1984 (Sec. 44) and corrupt insurance policies' PDSs involving third-party catastrophe clauses may deny the insured their legitimate rights for compensation of the additional benefits in the Building Insurance Valuation Schedule of Offer.

6.7 Advocacy for Harmonized Insurance Legislative Wording for Strata and General Home Insurance in Australia and Elsewhere and the Provision of a Contractual Building Insurance Valuation Report or Schedule of Values

I suggest that legislation covering both strata and non-strata building insurance be harmonized because non-strata general home insurance policies do not have a standard typical schedule of percentage values for all *other additional benefits* or extra costs or safety net. Those safety net promises could be reduced to zero with a "total loss" declaration by the insurer. This sad situation is likely to be a global phenomenon.

My suggestion is for the SSMA Act NSW 2015 and SSMR NSW 2016 Reg. 39—insurance replacement value cost formulation—to be used for both Strata and General Home Insurance Policies to comply with the make-up of costs formulation of the planned minimum replacement value immediately prior to the Event.

The reason for this is that the above legislation is the most accurate and advanced to date but could be improved substantially. Other states in Australia do not specify how the insurance value is planned! This deficiency apparently also applies globally. Use of online calculators is no substitute.

This is a fundamental error of other Australian states' strata legislation, and by extension, applies globally. Please check out your legislation to see if any BSI Value formulation method is described. I couldn't find any reference to it in the CCIOA Act of the State of Colorado in the United States.

Further, the Building Insurance Valuation Report Table should form part of, and be additional to, the various quotations shown in the Building Insurance Valuation Schedule of Offers with strata, or Schedule of Values with general home insurance policies.

When one of several offers is selected, this translates into the accepted Certificate of Insurance or Currency, forming the contract between the Owner/s and the Insurance provider.

The Report Table, or Schedule of Values, should depict both the *minimum Replacement Value immediately prior to the Event* AND the *100% of the catastrophe estimated full costs value*, and for those values to be individually, separately, and severally applicable.

By that I mean, in a *destruction, catastrophe, total loss, and constructive total loss* scenario, the additional benefits or extra costs linked to catastrophe condition, *are always payable* and can be separated from the total BSI Value and be claimed for use immediately by the owners for ancillary displacement costs.

That means that the *standardized* 15% Schedule value for *Loss of rent/temporary accommodation value* is immediately available to full value and should be paid out to the owners.

This would serve as a rebuttal to the inaccurate scenario in which the indemnity value is used by the loss adjuster to override the replacement value, and the costs of the asset are reduced until the evaluated, lower partial reinstatement value matches the BSI Value.

Longitude policy states:

> *We will not pay more than the indemnity value until a sum equal to the cost of reinstatement has been incurred.*

Why? Indemnity Value has nothing to do with real estate intangible asset value where insurance is based on Replacement Value.

At present, the Building Insurance Valuation Report is not a legally compulsory requirement, despite the legal framework suggesting that full insurance coverage is recommended. The statutory delineation of cost formulation fails to explicate the distinction between values, thereby placing the responsibility on the consumer to obtain comprehensive insurance coverage for replacement costs without definitive instruction on the precise expenditures that this value encompasses.

That is a typical mistake in legislative wording.

The legislation must stipulate the comprehensive costs that insurance policies for low-rise and high-rise constructions should include. The various Valuation Tables depicted in this publication show the respective formulations of value.

The estimated costs for the replacement value of building insurance are not exact amounts, but they help to reduce gap costs significantly.

Expenses such as ongoing mortgage costs, strata levies, and agency management fees are not usually reduced by the catastrophe or other event that cause displacement and are not accounted for in the calculation of full cost insurance replacement value. As gap costs, you would have to provide funding for these additional expenses.

6.8   Destruction, Catastrophe, Total Loss, and Constructive Total Loss Scenario, and the words "When New"

The following are my suggested additions to the SSMR 2016 NSW Regulations for when a *destruction, catastrophe, total loss, and constructive total loss* scenario prevails, and importantly, when partial or full loss or damage restoration occurs regarding the words "When New."

Use of the phrase "When New" must be eliminated from legislative language, as it suggests indemnity value based on original or past building costs that are unrelated to current and escalating costs in determining building insurance replacement value. The utilization of Replacement Value is exclusively appropriate for evaluating real estate value/s. The concept of the Indemnity Value pertains to movable property.

I suggest the following definitions:

- The terms Destruction, Catastrophe, and Total Loss are to be synonymous. The requirement of such a declaration by a third-party is deemed irrelevant.

Destruction, catastrophe, or total loss may occur because of one or another series of environmental Events listed in the policy wording, such as Fire, Earthquake, Tsunami, Storm Surge, Severe Storm Damage, or Flood.

- The term Constructive Total Loss refers to the condition that a Registered Structural Engineer has assessed, and an appropriate State Government Department has confirmed the total loss, and it requires the reinstatement or replacement of the affected structure/s on the existing site.
- If the value of the reinstatement or replacement valuation is equal to or exceeds 75% of the new re-build cost, as estimated by a Registered Quantity Surveyor, it would also trigger the payout for Constructive Total Loss.

An alternative compensation option is obtainable, whereby the property is sold, and the proprietors obtain a payment equal to the BSI Value. This encompasses the complete sums insured values for *catastrophe and loss of rent/temporary accommodation* as stated and exhibited in the Building Insurance Valuation Schedule of Offer or Schedule of Values.

It is imperative that we disburse these values based on the complete sums insured the policyholder paid in premiums. That the policy wording only covers expenses up to a certain amount, post-incurrence and after completion of costs, should not cause denial of the request.

This statement is premised on the fact that the BSI Value, which is provided as the payout, remains unused during the settlement offer that follows the insurer's declaration of "total loss."

It is not permissible to have two regulations functioning in conjunction that would discriminate against and nullify complete payments of insured sums. It is imperative that the law safeguards the insured—a task it is currently failing to perform adequately.

My recommendation is that the various above states of loss be explicitly specified in the legislation, using comparable phrasing as the text. This is because the Regulation does not expound on the circumstances that would activate supplementary benefits or expenses in a general home insurance policy or Contents insurance policy or strata residential/commercial insurance policy in quantifiable terms.

An instance of this circumstance concerning constructive total loss and a legal debacle is exemplified by the Botany edifices in Sydney—the OPAL and Mascot buildings. It may interest you to conduct an online search for that story.

6.9 The ICA General Code of Practice.

> *The General Insurance Code of Practice is a voluntary Code that protects the rights of policyholders.*

It is imperative to note that this statement is significantly inaccurate. The Code ensures the protection of the rights of its policy providers, while refraining from clarifying its aims and principles. Under the set objectives, insurers are expected to act with efficiency, fairness, and transparency when dealing with the insured.

The Code cannot safeguard the rights of the insured and is solely centered on the interests of the Policy Providers and their membership in the insurance industry.

The insurer generates a considerable conflict of interest by employing the ICA policy provision to define the condition of catastrophe in an insurance policy wording/PDS.

About the Code:

> *The Code sets out the standards that general insurers must meet when providing services to their customers, such as being honest.*

As of 2023, the absence of transparency and the lack of ASIC approval regarding the inclusion of a voluntary Code of Practice policy in any insurance policy wording/PDS continues to be prevalent.

> *The Code review process is there to ensure that the Code remains relevant and continues to meet the needs of consumers.*

Evidently, the ICA carried out these evaluations for internal use only, devoid of any input from informed consumers.

> *The Code raises customer service standards in the general insurance industry and protects the rights of consumers.*

The obligation to ensure the protection of rights lies with the policy providers, not with the consumers. The standards are not identical to the objectives and principles concerning the customer. In case of relevance, standards would aim at ensuring that additional expenses are uniformly considered in the PDSs of insurance policies.

> *These standards apply when selling insurance, dealing with insurance claims, **responding to catastrophes** and disasters, and handling complaints.*

Regardless of the standards, the details of each policy are always distinct. Regardless of the activation of the catastrophe clause in an insurance policy, the reaction to disasters is under the ICA Catastrophe

Code policy, ICA Board Declaration policy, or any other third-party state of emergency declaration clause associated with the State.

Note: Information in this section summarizes the catastrophe provisions in the Code. It is recommended that anyone who has experienced a catastrophe reviews **the Catastrophes** section in the Code (Section 9) for full details. Upon accessing the website, the term catastrophe pertains solely to Retail Insurance.

Catastrophes:

> *The Code of Practice commits insurers to respond to catastrophes efficiently, professionally, and compassionately.*

It is not advisable to have an external policy condition in place for the insurance contract to determine the contract terms efficiently. According to the Commonwealth Law Insurance Contract Act of 1984, it is neither efficient nor correct to include any wording in the policy or circumstance that pertains to a third-party, as the contract is only between the insurer and the insured.

This clause not only cannot protect the insured's rights but also denies them any rights they may have had regarding the Building Valuation Schedule Offer and the Certificate of Insurance, as well as the insured sum values specified and exemplified in the Schedule and/or Certificate or the wording in its PDS.

> *The ICA will declare an event to be a catastrophe when it results in many claims and involves multiple insurers.*

The conclusion is diabolical and is far removed from the meaning of a catastrophic situation, which involves destruction, total loss, and constructive total loss. The current unfortunate situation may persist due to the lack of approval of the Code by ASIC and the absence of any legislative framework defining terms such as destruction, catastrophe, total loss, or constructive total loss.

> *A catastrophe is most declared after an extreme weather event such as a severe cyclone, bushfire, flood, or storm.*

It should be noted that the events listed are not exhaustive of all defined events outlined in any insurance policy wording/PDS, and it is possible for loss, damage, or destruction, or constructive total loss to occur, regardless of whether a Catastrophe Code declaration or ICA Board Declaration has been made.

The exclusion of Home Building Insurance and Contents Insurance from the Insurance Council of Australia's jurisdiction is justifiable. This is due to the ICA's intervention in Third-Party Catastrophe Clause policies, which have resulted in a conflict of interest.

The determinations and terms established by the ICA, coupled with its policies, do not form a legal insurance policy/PDS condition provision, nor do they constitute a valid entity in any Home Building Insurance or Contents Insurance policy contract wording. This is not a legal interpretation, but a practical and commonsense one.

Longitude, a major Stratum residential insurance provider, employs a different catastrophe clause terminology—a state declaration of a state of emergency.

The Youi Home insurance policy states openly that it does not employ the ICA Code of Practice, although it is a signatory of the ICA Code of Practice.

To put it briefly, the ICA Catastrophe Code displays a considerable tendency and has the potential to have an adverse impact on the policyholders. It represents a significant conflict of interest within the insurance provider industry because the additional benefits outlined in the policy are directly affected by both the ICA Catastrophe Code and the ICA Board Declaration, and the cover-holder may also be implicated if they comply with Lloyd's directives and cannot protect against conflicts of interest.

My advocacy is for ASIC to mandate the ICA Code of Practice as a prerequisite for its approval and oversight. The aim is to eliminate the catastrophe clause definition or declaration by the ICA from being present in any policy wording, including any State-based catastrophe clause that pertains to a state of emergency and/or state-authorized evacuation announcement.

This is because the conditional meaning and application of a policy's catastrophe condition and related additional benefits and compensation costs have an adverse effect on the consumer.

The provisions also encompass the deduction of any financial benefits furnished by the State. It is not the policy of the State to provide subsidies to insurance providers.

Don't wait for ASIC to change this appalling situation. My suggestion to combat the denial of payment for the additional benefits is to obtain insurance coverage for **100% of the catastrophe estimated full costs BSI Value.**

6.10 The Basis of Settlement of Claims[22]

Please refer, if you like, to the policy referenced in the footnote. Extracts are shown from **Longitude** S.1 cl.8.1 (Basis of Settlement of Claims):

Cl. 8. Basis of Settlement of Claims

Note: I'll explain what the reasoning of "extra cost" means below.

> *Unless otherwise shown in the Policy Schedule, claims will be settled based on Reinstatement or Replacement and Extra Cost:*

---

22 https://www.longitudeinsurance.com.au/app/uploads/2023/01/ResidentialStrataInsurancePolicyWordingPDSFINAL15.10.2021.pdf

Cl 8.1 Reinstatement or Replacement means:

a) where Your Insured Property is physically lost or destroyed, with Buildings, the rebuilding of it, or with Insured Property other than Buildings, the replacement of it, by similar property, in either case in a condition equal to but not better or more extensive than its condition when new.

b) where Your Insured Property is damaged, the repair of the damage and the restoration of the damaged portion of Your Insured Property to a condition substantially the same as but not better or more extensive than its condition when new.

Note: It is not the responsibility of the insurer to rebuild the premises, but it should repair and reinstate partial damage. The rebuild part is the prerogative of the insured.

Cl. 8.2 Extra Cost:

We will also pay the extra cost of reinstatement, including demolition or dismantling of Your Insured Property incurred to comply with the requirements, operative at the time of reinstatement.

Note: Extra costs for reinstatement described above are **not** extra costs as they are costed into the BSI Value. The supposed extra costs of Demolition and Architect Fees and Charges would not be paid if the BSI Value is otherwise exhausted. If the building is not rebuilt, the BSI Value would not be exhausted and should be paid out in full.

The words, under the wording "Basis of Settlement of Claims" — "Unless otherwise shown in the Policy Schedule," are highly misleading and not transparent, as the Additional Benefits—*the extra costs for sums insured in the policy schedule*—are not included in the reasoning of extra costs. They are not covered under the insurer's basis of settlement of claims.

Having read that, we need to step back a bit and review the Catastrophe clause, where the *other extra costs stated in the Schedule* for Additional Benefits (B) apply for a declared catastrophe by an external third-party.

Cl. 5.1 Catastrophe Cover:

> *If the physical loss, destruction, or damage to Your Insured Property under Section 1 is due to a Catastrophe, or another insured Event occurring within 72 hours after a Catastrophe, which occurs during the Period of Insurance:*
>
> a) *We will pay up to the amount or percentage noted in Your Policy Schedule for Catastrophe Cover for Increased Costs You incur directly associated with or because of the Catastrophe.*

Note: Catastrophe cover in this policy (Longitude) is initially invoked by a third-party through the State declaration of a state of emergency. It then covers the Schedule values for *catastrophe* **and** *loss of rent/temporary accommodation* sums insured values.

To submit a claim for building costs and displacement expenses, it is necessary to have incurred such expenses during the policy's validity period. The philosophy in question is both counterintuitive and unjust, as it necessitates bearing the expenses for building restoration and displacement without any monetary support from the policy. What was the purpose of obtaining insurance?

If rebuilding is not desired, the only way to combat this injustice is to insure for *100% of the catastrophe full costs BSI Value*, to get the value for displacement expenses and other costs.

> *This Additional Benefit extends the Sum Insured or other limits under this Section 1 by the amount or percentage noted in Your Policy Schedule for:*
>
> *– Insured Property; and*
>
> *– all other Additional Benefits in this Section 1, but only if Your Insured Property is reinstated or replaced.*

The funds allocated for loss of rent or temporary accommodation expenses, as outlined in the Schedule of Sums Insured values, are also currently unavailable. These funds are set at 15% of the BSI Value.

> *We will not pay more than the Increased Costs actually incurred by You. We will not pay any amount under this Additional Benefit until the relevant Sum Insured or other applicable limits shown next to Buildings and Common Contents under this Section 1, as shown in the Schedule, have been exhausted.*

The rationale in question is not related to Common Contents, as that value would fall under either Contents or Landlords insurance policy. Alternatively, *common areas contents requiring work value* should have been costed into the BSI Value itself by a competent valuer, and *common contents* not listed in the Building Valuation Schedule of Offer by an incompetent Broker.

> *b) where a Lot that is destroyed or damaged due to the Catastrophe is occupied as a residence by the Lot Owner, We will pay for the Cost of Evacuation incurred by the Lot Owner, or any person permanently residing with the Lot Owner immediately prior to the happening of the Catastrophe, following an order for evacuation issued by a public or statutory authority, entity or person empowered by law to issue such an order due to the happening of the Catastrophe.*

The amount payable will be reduced by any compensation payable by any public or statutory authority. The most We will pay for the Cost of Evacuation is 1% of the Sum Insured in total for all Lot Owners per Catastrophe.

Taxpayers don't fund insurance money, and it's not a replacement for money from the insurer.

For this Additional Benefit only, the following additional definitions apply:

- *Catastrophe means any occurrence that gives rise to the declaration by the relevant authority of a state of emergency affecting the area in which the buildings are situated.*

- *Cost of Evacuation means the costs incurred for any form of transport to the designated place of evacuation and subsequent return to the Location to resume permanent residency.*

- *Increased Costs means:*

i) for Insured Property—the difference between the cost of reinstatement or replacement actually incurred under the Basis of Settlement provisions of this Section 1 and the cost of reinstatement or replacement that would have applied had the Catastrophe not occurred. [Work that one out? Reinstatement or replacement means rebuild.]

ii) for the Additional Benefits—the difference between the amount payable for the costs, expenses, fees, or other charges covered by the Additional Benefits and that which would have been payable had the Catastrophe not occurred. [Work that one out? How long does the insured have to wait in order to claim expenses when the contract validity is 12 months only?]

> *This Additional Benefit applies provided that the Sum Insured under Section 1 represents no less than 80% of the cost of reinstatement or replacement immediately prior to the Catastrophe. [The contract document does not explicitly mention the cost of reinstatement or replacement prior to the Catastrophe.]*

In summary, the above discusses the impracticality of interpreting Increased Costs and the incalculable expenses before and after a disaster, along with the hypothetical costs that would have been involved if the disaster had not taken place. The definition of catastrophe aligns with the one outlined in the policy PDS.

The cruncher is the 80% Average Provision Rule, which I have explained is unworkable.

This policy and others that apply the 80% Average Provision Rule are covered by the Insurance Contract Act 1984 (Commonwealth) Sec. 44, which I assert is unworkable for real estate applications and needs reform.

That declared catastrophe clause—Longitude cl.5.1—has multiple conditions and limitations of which you should know. If none of these conditions and limitations are operative, you will get no Additional Benefits for Catastrophe Schedule value or Loss of rent/temporary accommodation Schedule value.

With Reinstatement and Replacement, it means **full** reinstatement or replacement, but where partial reinstatement or replacement occurs, the Indemnity Value valuation will be the case until the spent value reaches the BSI Value. That is a false dictum.

Where a total loss is declared, only the BSI Value would be payable, and the contract then ended. That means that those **extra costs** could hardly ever be included in the payout, as they have not been spent. This is because the contract has been ended and the BSI Value paid out.

The only way to combat this injustice and get full compensation for the additional benefits is to insure *100% of the catastrophe estimated full costs BSI Value*, where the extra costs are built into this value.

Lawmakers and Regulators should pay special attention to the Longitude Catastrophe clause wording in Section 1 Cl 5.1.

I say the insurance doctrine of incurred costs for the additional benefits outlined in the Schedule is illogical, impractical, and unworkable.

Longitude possibly represents the worst conditions and limitations of any policy and you, the insured, can never obtain the additional benefits stated and paid for in the Schedule.

6.11 Repeal of the Valuers Act 2003[23]

In NSW, the repeal of the Valuers Act 2003 was repealed on 1 March 2016. This brought about a new situation and the repeal means that property valuers in NSW no longer need to be registered. All **registered valuers** became **qualified valuers**, and for them to become members of one of the Property Institutes, such as API/RICS and AVI.

None of these members should provide services for strata residential schemes of three or more lots on one site and title, under the API Code. API says all valuers should be a member of the API, and the IVSC only recognizes the API as a Valuation Professional Organization.

Was the NSW Productivity Commission's decision to repeal the Act based on a comprehensive evaluation of the situation? Or was their reasoning limited to the assumption that the calculation of insurance value is simply a matter of adding up costs, leading to a reduction in expenses for consumers by eliminating the need for a Registered Valuer? What would be the final expense borne by the insured who received an inaccurate insurance valuation report which only insured

---

23 https://legislation.nsw.gov.au/view/html/inforce/current/act-2003-004

them for the base replacement value and failed to cover all the associated expenses and costs for the necessary duration?

The repeal has led to concern in the Real Estate Industry.[24]

> *REINSW sees a role for the professional bodies working co-operatively with government for the oversight of compliance with the regulatory environment and the maintenance of professional standards. While industry must be involved in the process of regulation, it alone should not be solely responsible.*

6.12 Legislation Causing Adverse Effects for the Insured

These **adverse effects** include:

(i) ***Catastrophe clause.*** Legislation describing *destruction, catastrophe, total loss,* and *constructive total loss* is missing.

(ii) ***The 80% Average Provision Rule.*** The Insurance Contracts Act 1984 (Commonwealth) Sec. 44 clause outlines the application of this Rule. This clause is impractical and unworkable for determining the Replacement Value of real estate.

(iii) ***Insurance Schedule.*** This is the Building Insurance Valuation Schedule of Offer that contains unnecessary Section Line Items, causing higher premium values for nothing—and for which both Strata Managers and brokers do not first get the clients' requirements, through filling out a *proforma schedule form,* but produce a standardized schedule of values that can be dissimilar and include unnecessary or inaccurate line-item values. The line items of the Schedule are not properly stated by legislation and

---

24 https://www.urban.com.au/news/deregulation-of-valuing-industry-a-concern-reinsw

many of the items listed may never be used, as they are only valid during the contract period.

(iv) ***Third-party Beneficiary Clause.*** This is the Insurance Contracts Act 1984 (Commonwealth) Sec. 48 clause, where a third-party **person** can claim off the insured's policy for injury, damage, and/or death, and even **non-persons**, such as credit providers (Banks/financiers), can claim any outstanding mortgage or loan from the policy value without the consent of the insured in whose name the policy was taken out, thus potentially rendering the insurance value to zero.

(v) ***Online calculators offered by an agency.*** The discontinuance of these calculators is necessary for formulating the replacement value of the property to be insured. As a result of the likely underinsurance due to the replacement value calculation, the insured will incur considerable out-of-pocket expenses, given that the minimum replacement valuation excludes the costs of increased building expenses and temporary housing for 104 weeks or more.

6.13 Definition of Insurance Valuer and Replacement Value

To this day, a definitive description of a Valuer cannot be found in any legal documentation, including the most recent DBP Act NSW 2020. The IVSC has not yet reached a conclusion on the definitions of Insurance Valuer and Replacement Value, resulting in a state of confusion.

Lawmakers, please take note.

The Meaning of Residential Property Insurance Valuer

Under part (f) of the API Code of Practice, the meaning of Residential Property Insurance Valuer **does NOT include** regarding Code cl. (f) (vi): An insurance valuation on behalf of an Owners' Corporation for a Strata Scheme; and (f) (ix): Common property within a residential Strata Scheme.

The reader may refer now to the Revised Code.[25]

For Version 3, dated 6 December 2021, Refer to 2.4. Unsuitable/Out of Scope. This refers to the API and the Australian Banking and Finance Industry Residential Valuation Standing Instructions Version 3 effective date 6 December 2021.

6.14 A Residential Building Insurance Valuer

A residential building insurance valuer has a **responsibility way beyond** that required for valuing a set of teacups or general property types, things, articles, or machinery. Valuers who are members of the AVI or RICS-associated and qualified API certified members who provide strata residential building insurance reports or valuations are not adequately equipped to perform this task.

The complexity of this matter is further compounded by the terms and standards of the IVSC. As of 2023, the definitions of Replacement Value and the conditions and connotations for real estate property insurance valuation purposes have yet to be resolved and defined by registered specialist insurance valuer practitioners.

In Australian legislation, the terminology Replacement Value is frequently used, which signifies the minimum replacement value right before the occurrence of the Event.

---

[25] https://www.api.org.au/wp-content/uploads/2021/08/ABFI-Residential-Valuation-Standing-Instructions_Version3_effective-6-Dec-2021.pdf

This value does not account for full costs being **ancillary extra costs** associated with repair, reinstatement, replacement, rebuild, or replacement on another site.

There is a possibility of increased construction expenses due to damage, disasters, complete loss, and constructive total loss, as well as expenses related to loss of rent or temporary accommodation. Other significant expenses may include extended accommodation costs and local council site-related planning requirements, along with their estimated code compliance provisions. This is especially relevant for high-rise buildings.

Owners of high-rise structures who insure for the replacement value amount **only** will incur exceptionally large **out-of-pocket gap costs**.

Words such as *"we will pay for temporary accommodation from the time you can't live in your home until you get back to your home,"* are **misleading**. Also, *"we will pay for temporary accommodation for **up to** 12 months,"* is **misleading**, as there may also be a percentage value of the BSI Value attached to that, say 25% or otherwise stated, and the lesser value of the two prevails.

Where a complete 25% safety net or comparable gap coverage is assured in home insurance, the value of such coverage may amount to zero if the insurer declares a total loss and only pays out the BSI value. Failure to enhance the BSI Value as recommended will cause gap costs on your part.

With strata residential building insurance, the additional benefits or percentage escalation values for ancillary extra costs are treated differently by different policies, but may also amount to zero, where a total loss is declared, and the BSI Value only is paid out.

That is why the insured should always insure at least *100% of the catastrophe estimated full costs BSI Value* every time to avoid underinsurance.

6.15 The Definition of a Certified Practicing Valuer

The API Code of Conduct is quite exhaustive and explanatory, but the AVI Code is not so generous.

I believe the AVI is purposely very cunning with its choice of similar wording and designation of the qualification acronym "CPV" to make it directly comparable and competitive with the API so that Strata Managers and others employing them do not understand or appreciate the differences in quality.

They would therefore not be aware of the more extensive tertiary accredited educational standards required for the API CPV qualification and API restriction applicable to strata building insurance valuation.

There are three Valuation Property Institutes: API, RICS, and AVI.

6.16 The Residential Valuation Industry Group (RVI) V.3[26]

The ABFI Residential Insurance Valuation Standing Instructions are very confusing.

The instruction appears to encompass various types of residential valuations, including both strata and non-strata, without clear differentiation in the standing instructions. In 2023, neither the API nor NSW Fair Trading has taken any action regarding the matter.

The revised version, RVI V3, which came into effect on 1 October 2019, replaces the ABFI Residential Valuation Standing Instructions Version 2.2.1.

Valuers are required to complete that module every year for their ongoing requirements.

I am interested in the following Exclusions:

---

[26] https://www.api.org.au/wp-content/uploads/2021/08/ABFI-Residential-Valuation-Standing-Instructions_Version3_effective-6-Dec-2021.pdf

cl. 2.4, Unsuitable / Out of Scope.

    n. Properties with three or more approved dwellings on one title (e.g., houses, flats, units, and villas).

    o. Any non-residential property, including office, retail or industrial.

    q. Mixed use properties (e.g., shop and residence - note: this does not refer to residential properties in a mixed-use zoning or home occupations).

    u. Residential property, where in the Valuer's opinion, the market value exceeds $5 million.

cl. 3.6, Replacement Insurance Estimate.

Provide a cost estimate for building insurance. The estimate should include the current replacement cost and allowances for:

    a. Demolition, removal of debris and clearing of the site for reconstruction.

    b. All professional fees.

    c. Council and other statutory fees and charges.

    d. An escalation allowance on all costs through the insured year from the valuation date.

Note: Values for (d) **on all costs** throughout the insured year from the valuation date are **not correct**. They are incomplete, as they do not show how the make-up of escalation value is calculated in the first escalation period in relation to the site inspection/valuation date and the policy expiration date, and the second escalation period of at least 104 weeks for ancillary costs and expenses after the policy expiration date, for low-rise buildings.

The escalation period in (d) is **not accurate** in that there are two escalation periods, calculated differently for low-rise and high-rise applications. Please refer to Table 4.1 and Table 4.3 as a guide.

A **Certified Practicing Valuer** is a person who, by education, training, and experience, is qualified to perform a valuation of real property.

This obviously requires legal clarification of the requirements for a "Qualified Valuer" to provide for the provision of a residential, or otherwise, **building insurance valuation**—whether for strata or non-strata application.

It is patently clear that Strata Managing agencies do not appreciate the requirements for the professional who may be licensed to provide the Strata Building Insurance Valuation Reports and Capital Works Reports, and who consistently bypass the services of the Registered Quantity Surveyor in favor of the unqualifying services provided by members of the API, resulting in the continued phenomenon of underinsurance, which is **highly potentially prejudicial** to the insured.

6.17 The Acquisition of Capital Works Reports and Storage of Annual Financial Statements

The acquisition of Capital Works Reports, commonly known as the 10-year plan, requires the development of a Stratum Financial Plan. This plan must show the accounting of receipts and expenditures for both the Administrative Fund and the Capital Works Fund over the financial period for each year, as well as for the next 10 years, in order to meet regulatory requirements. This is because the planned or collected strata levies, also referred to as receipts or assessments, need to be allocated to both the Administrative Fund and the Capital Works Fund (formerly known as the sinking fund).

The utilisation of digitised financial statements is also helpful in revealing past expenditures, which can aid in predicting future expenses, specifically for continuous or recurrent maintenance tasks such as surface painting, among other things. In older strata schemes, let's say one that is over 15 years old, should not cause spending on acquiring a capital works plan, since historical expenses are readily accessible.

In order to effectively plan for major expenses, it is recommended to obtain quotations based on engineering or architectural specifications at least two years prior. This will allow for confirmation of the expected funding value, accounting for additional inflation up to the year of expenditure.

With the framework outlining the annual financial statements outlining the receipts and expenses in the chart schedule, it is imperative to also develop a Levy Valuation Schedule. This schedule will outline the receipts required to populate the forward chart schedule.

This is where the art of calculating values required to be paid into each Fund needs to be evaluated and the annual rate increase may differ between the Funds.

The Levy Valuation Schedule must accurately depict the quarterly deposits, or any other determinations, to be allocated to each fund. The utilization of scientific or strategic planning skills is paramount in this scenario, as it entails the computation of the estimated levy for every upcoming year and subsequently dividing these cumulative amounts between the Administrative Fund and the Capital Works Fund.

It is advisable to conduct regular reviews of the financial plan, ideally more frequently than every 5 years, in order to make necessary adjustments to levy rates. As part of my regular procedure, I would obtain rates from the Levy Valuation Schedule, ensuring a minimum of three years for their subsequent presentation and approval at the AGM.

Implementing this measure ensures that rates for a single year cannot be carried forward without change until a later AGM, thus preventing the opportunity to capitalise on the initial cost increase at the start of the financial period. The lack of logical reasoning in Sections 79 and 81 of the NSW Strata Act is highlighted by this strategy, as it cannot recognise the fiscal inflation between consecutive years.

I also strongly recommend that any financial year period that is not in accord with a calendar year be changed to coincide with a calendar year, so that rates' increases start at the beginning of the year to take maximum advantage of fiscal inflation increases immediately.

An increase in levy value is usually in accord with the most recent BPI inflation rate. Up to 20 years, say before 2019, the *median* residential building inflation rate of the eight capital cities in Australia was 4.5% according to Corelogic[27] for general housing, but the Sydney rate was usually higher, say about 5%. The regular rate of increase was disrupted during the Covid-19 pandemic, thus causing adjustments to the levy rates to address any deficiencies in rates planning. How many treasurers have done that, I wonder?

It should be noted; however, that current rental rates have a direct bearing on the BSI value and its ability to provide for rental accommodation after the Event. Sydney's median rent jumped in the last quarter of 2023 to $750 per week according to figures from Prop Track.

That means that leasing a house in Sydney is now 36% dearer than in Melbourne, Australia's second largest city.

Based on my extensive experience in formulating long-term financial plans, I have observed that plans exceeding 5 years are increasingly inaccurate. The major cause of this can be attributed to the difficulty in accurately predicting future inflation rates, which include both CPI and BPI variables. To tackle this matter, it is vital to review the forward plan more frequently than every 5 years, highlighting the pressure and cost factors in the absence of a designated person within the owners corporation, as previously stated.

Another distraction I have found is that external valuers usually place excess funds into term deposits. This practice can interfere with timely access to funds when immediately required. Any interest earned on fixed term deposits should not be planned into the unnecessary Capital

---

27   https://www.corelogic.com.au/__data/assets/pdf_file/0018/19161/CoreLogic-HVI-Nov2023-FINAL.pdf

Works Plan, but treated as a revenue bonus and added to the amount of receipts in any year and shown as another line item of receipts.

6.18 RICS Professional Standards, Australia RICS Valuation—Global Standards 2017: Australia National Supplement.[28]

Part 2 Valuation standards

Overview

> 1   This document assists valuers who are members of RICS, including those who are also members of the Australian Property Institute (API), in ensuring that a valuation undertaken under Red Book Global Edition also complies with the Australia and New Zealand Valuation and Property Standards (ANZVPS).[29]

Note: Notwithstanding the RICS Red Book Global Edition, RICS operates in Australia under the auspices of the API, under reciprocity arrangements, and needs to comply with the API Standards and code of conduct.

It is lamentable that the IVSC does not yet have a position on the meaning of Replacement Value for insurance of Real Estate Property or Valuer for building insurance Replacement Value, or for estimated full costs insurance value of Real Estate Property.

The prohibition or discontinuance of calculators for determining the BSI Value is necessary not just in Australia but globally. The reason being that they are not precise in providing the full costs or even the base replacement value which will suffice after the Event. I would

---

28   RICS Valuation - Global Standards 2017 - Australia National Supplement (PDF 2.54MB) Published date: 08 August 2019

29   https://www.rics.org/profession-standards/rics-standards-and-guidance/sector-standards/valuation-standards/red-book/red-book-global

like to direct your attention to Chapter 4, Table 4.1, to corroborate this assertion.

The SSMR NSW Reg. 39 places homeowners seeking general home building insurance at a disadvantage—the general home insurance value isn't included in the NSW legislation for at least the minimum replacement value estimate, and the percentage sums for safety nets and extra costs don't match the Strata Building Insurance Valuation Schedule of Offer terms.

There's no standard for extra costs values in home building insurance, so policies can differ in what extra costs they cover. In the event of a total loss, the insurer will declare the BSI Value and pay that sum out, but the percentage value or term period for extra costs may end right away.

I strongly recommend that all States/Territories adhere to the NSW Strata Insurance Legislation, at a minimum, and ultimately strive for a uniform National Building Insurance Valuation Code.

I am also a proponent of the IVSC improving their definition of the formulation of the structure of insurance costs and interpreting insurance appraiser for both strata and general home ownership applications.

The adoption of the method for calculating the BSI Value, as illustrated in Chapter 4 of the Building Valuation Tables, could be considered by all nations.

6.19 The Case for the Discontinuance of the Use of Calculators Worldwide

In so far as building insurance Calculators are concerned, they should be discontinued because they cannot:

- Include the obligatory site visit walkthrough/walk around.

- Have any required date and time-stamped photographs taken at the time of inspection and valuation of the insured property. The API Code requires at least two photos.

- Assess any site-specific hazardous circumstances, such as location, asbestos, cladding type, fire, and safety systems.

- Provide the obligatory council visit to check on statutory rules and control plans.

- Account accurately for the total building's gross area, including owner's fixtures, fittings, and improvements to common property.

- Produce an accurate estimate of the common area's contents requiring work, including recreational fixtures, fittings, and other site environmental improvements to be included in the sum insured.

- Account accurately for the type and quality of existing building construction or building improvements planned for completion within the period of insurance, as a claim may be made on the last day of the current period of insurance; typically, a dollar value is placed on this requirement.

- Calculate accurately the escalation costs both at the forefront of the calculation and the escalation costs at the backend of the calculation.

- Judge accurately for the costs of Architect Fees and Charges based on the total cost of the works or estimate properly for the site clearance costs.

- Relate to any insurance policy wording/PDS the prospective Insured may use.

- Enable an estimate of the 100% Catastrophe Estimated Full Costs BSI Value and other local council statutory planning requirements estimated costs to obviate underinsurance over the perceived replacement period for 104 weeks, as described in the NSW statutory valuation formulation method, for low-rise buildings.

As explained in Chapter 4, the initial requirement after the Event, which makes it impossible to inhabit your residence, is to secure alternative accommodation. As mentioned earlier, the present rental values have a direct influence on the BSI value and the funding for a minimum duration of 104 weeks for low-rise and 208 weeks for high-rise accommodation. The calculation of Replacement Value, whether done by a calculator or by other means, does not take this into consideration.

Is there any wonder a Calculator cannot provide an honest, accurate, and transparent estimate for estimated full costs?

6.20 Lot Owners' Fittings, Fixtures, and Improvements

I say that structural improvements and additions, internal improvements, and refurbishments, and improving the quality of fixtures or finishes, increase the value of the lot's common area.

Referring to Longitude sec. 1 cl. 2.6.

 a) *Any item or structure for the exclusive use of a Lot Owner and which is permanently attached to or fixed to the building defined as common area, to become legally part of it.*

b) *Any improvements made to an existing part of the Building by a Lot Owner for their exclusive use Section 1 Property: Physical Loss, Destruction or Damage, provided that the Lot Owners' Fixtures and Improvements were newly gained, installed, or constructed within the three years prior to:*

  i) *Your most recent renewal; or*

  ii) *Your most recent insurance valuation, whichever is the earlier.*

This should be the most recent renewal only because, unfortunately, the **Insurance Valuation Report** does not form part of the insurance contract documents and may also be up to five years old.

The Insurance Valuation Report is currently only provided to show to the broker the BSI Value to source comparative quotations.

That insurance valuation does not show specifically or expressly any Lot Owners' fixtures, fittings, and improvements, as that value is, or should be, included in the base BSI Value—as per the NSW Strata Act and regulations, for at least the minimum insurance replacement value formulation cost structure. This accounts for the total gross building's value, including common areas contents requiring work value.

Section 1 Cl 3.10 (b) of the above policy (Longitude) refers to **internal improvements**. These increase the quality and value of the building, for which the Insurance Valuer/Registered Quantity Surveyor would not value when assessing the total updated value of the lot under the timeframes 2.6 b (i) and (ii), as the insurance valuer is unlikely to do a walkthrough of every lot in the Scheme as the cost factor to do that is commercially non-viable.

The upshot of this is that the NSW SSMA Act 2015 is incorrect in specifying that any improvements made to an existing part of the buildings by a Lot Owner for their exclusive use **may**, repeat *may*, require a by-law for their maintenance and repair or replacement.

This statement is deemed incorrect if deemed necessary, since the Owners' Corporation manages maintenance and repair of communal property, and its insurance policy extends to all contents of common areas in need of repair, including assets attached to the building for exclusive use. Therefore, the law in question may be counterproductive for two reasons:

(i) It **may impose** extra unnecessary costs on the Lot Owner for sourcing a by-law for Owners' Corporation approval at an AGM **when all by-law costs** are for the Owners' Corporation's account.

(ii) The Owners' Corporation insurance covers *all areas of common areas contents requiring work, including all Lot Owners' fixtures and fittings and internal improvements* carried out within the timeframes specified by, for example, Longitude 2.6 Lot Owners' Fixtures and Improvements.

The legislation does not include any provision for exempting specific components of the common areas contents of the Owners' Corporation from the comprehensive insurance policy. By illustration, those areas designated only for the use of each individual Lot Owner.

Once the Lot Owners' fixtures, fittings and improvements are in place, they remain so and are covered by the Owners' Corporation's insurance, which is renewed annually, as required by legislation.

With **partial loss/damage** or **total loss** or **constructive total loss** of the property, the insurance policy would cover those additional fixtures, fittings, and improvements, as all values thereof are **included in the Base BSI Value of the policy in force**, as they are *prescribed to be* per the NSW Strata Act 2015.

It is the obligation of the Owners' Corporation to ensure the maintenance and upkeep of the fixtures, fittings, and improvements of Lot Owners, despite the existence of a by-law that is needless, unfeasible, and impractical, which states that Lot Owners handle the same, if they agree to such a by-law, which is not advisable.

I assert, however, that there is no one rule that fits all.

Where proprietors of lots wish to acquire extra common spaces, they ought to first consult with the strata committee and subsequently seek the guidance of a strata attorney to guarantee legal compliance. This may involve registering a contract and by-law. The expenses may be transferred to the proprietor of the lot.

The Owners' Corporation holds the responsibility of ensuring that Lot Owners' fixtures, improvements or applications for additional common area acquisition conform to the standards established by the Owners' Corporation.

6.21 Deficiency of Australian States' and Territory Strata Titles Acts

I repeat here my concerns regarding their deficiency.

The formulation of costs does not include both the *minimum insurance replacement value immediately prior to the Event* and the *100% catastrophe estimated full costs replacement value* for consideration.

Insufficient insurance coverage arising from this situation might cause substantial financial losses or the need for additional payments to cover the shortfall, should the BSI Value fail to fully cover the costs related to repairing, replacing, or rebuilding the structure, as well as ongoing living expenses. This may affect the availability and value of additional expenses with minimum insurance replacement value.

Initially, it may not be possible to compensate for replacement statutory fees and expenses, such as Architect Fees and Charges, and Debris Removal costs, if the BSI Value is underinsured and already depleted.

Second, if the BSI Value is not augmented to include escalated building replacement costs and Lot Owners' displacement costs and expenses, there is a possibility that these expenses may not be payable. Therefore, the BSI minimum replacement value needs to be increased by at least 30%.

The expenses related to displacement include loss of rent, temporary accommodation costs, *extended* accommodation expenses in high-rise buildings, other potential costs, and ancillary local council statutory estimated planning costs for a rebuild on that site.

The Public Liability Insurance Value should be $20m in line with the NSW Strata regulations.

There is no legal definition of destruction, catastrophe, total loss, and constructive total loss.

Unfortunately, there is no available description outlining the required skills or competencies for the position of *Building Insurance Valuation Specialist Valuer Practitioner*, except for the State of Queensland. In Queensland, it is commendable to have either a registration as a Quantity Surveyor or as a valuer.

Because of the repeal of the Valuers Act of 2003 in March 2016, there is currently an absence of valuers registered with the Government in NSW.

6.22 Suggested Documents to include in the Building Insurance Package

There is no description of what all the documents comprising the building insurance documentation package ***should include***, namely:

   a. **The Certificate of Insurance**—states who the insured are and who the underwriters are and their respective portions of responsibility for the insured sum/s value/s.

   b. **The Building Insurance Valuation Schedule of Offers**— three offers are usually required, or reasons are to be provided by the broker why three quotes could not be provided.

c. **An insurance proforma, filled out by the strata committee treasurer**—of the desired line items in the Valuation Schedule of Offers, is not required to be provided first by the building's Managing Agent/Strata Manager or the broker, and this creates unnecessary line items that potentially increase the insurance premium.

d. **The Building Insurance Valuation Estimation Report**—which, as stated, should not be older than five years and the BSI Value maintained or adjusted annually.

Including the original or current Building Insurance Valuation Report in the contractual documentation is deemed obligatory, along with its presentation in the AGM Agenda and Minutes as a point of reference for the values established by a Registered Specialist Building Insurance Valuer Practitioner. The report must include the minimum replacement value estimation immediately before the Event, as well as the 100% of the catastrophe estimated full cost value, or the *greater extended value* for high-rise complexes.

The above suggestions have *not* been properly and definitively addressed in any legislation.

Evidence shows that understanding insurance becomes more complex due to the enactment of Strata Titles Acts and Strata Building Insurance legislation by other Australian States and Territories.

POSTSCRIPT

It has been a pleasure producing this work and I trust that having gained this insurance guide, you now have the information to enable you to select the correct BSI Value.

I sincerely hope that lawmakers will pay attention to correcting adverse legislation—or at least make the legislative improvement suggestions come to fruition so that insurance policies can truly be honest, transparent, and nonprejudicial, and so that justice for the insured can be restored.

Thank you for acquiring this book. *Non Scholae Sed Vitae*—Quote by philosopher Lucius Annaeus Seneca the Younger: "*We do not learn for school, but for life.*"

ACKNOWLEDGEMENTS

I would like to acknowledge the following for their assistance in the production of this work-

Manuscript critique: Stephanee Killen, Integrative Ink

Substantive Edit: Stephanee Killen, Integrative Ink

Copyedit: Stephanee Killen, Integrative Ink

Proofread: Tina Morganella, Reedsy

Cover Design: Jennifer Stimson, Reedsy

Interior Design: Jennifer Stimson, Reedsy

Website Design: Kathryn Fitzgerald, Reesy

www.ingramcontent.com/pod-product-compliance
Lightning Source LLC
Chambersburg PA
CBHW051436290426
44109CB00016B/1576